Surviving Shadows: Holocaust Trauma Unveiled

Nathan Lynn

TABLE OF CONTENTS

continued

continued

LIST OF FIGURES

CHAPTER I
INTRODUCTION

Two opposing viewpoints exist in the literature regarding coping with and recovery from trauma -- *talking is therapeutic*, and *talking impedes healing*. The answer, while passionately argued by opposite sides of the trauma field, may ultimately be told by the survivors themselves, who have endured periods of both silence and expression. By listening to Holocaust survivors who were traumatized as children, we could learn more about the two sides of the debate and the role of silence and expression in coping.

Expressing vs. Avoiding

The notion of the healing power of talking about and "working through" trauma is not new. Originally seen in the earliest empirically recorded treatment of trauma, it continues to be *en vogue* as the prevalent trauma treatment more than a century later (Herman, 1992; Summerfield, 2000). Therapists adhering to a variety of different theoretical assumptions operate from this theory of integration (that to face down and incorporate trauma through the psyche's exposure to the traumatic event characterizes the pathway to recovery) (e.g., Cook, Spinazzola, Ford, Lanktree, et al., 2005).

Recently, however, empirical evidence of the null or detrimental effects of trauma expression requires a re-examination of this idea that integration leads to healing. Some (e.g. Bonanno, 2004) argue that avoidance is more effective than dwelling on past trauma. Avoidance may actually facilitate adaptation. While compelling cases have similarly been made by others, (e.g., Ginzburg, Solomon, & Bleich, 2002; Gist & Devilly, 2002; McNally, Bryant, & Ehlers, 2003; Spiro, Shalev, Solomon and Kotler, 1989), most practitioners in the trauma field have ignored or dismissed this evidence. The general public, however, has shown interest in this alternative view; "avoiders" have received recent attention in newspapers and radio programs (e.g., NPR "Face the Nation" 8/22/06; Slater, L., New York Times 2/23/03; Spiegel, A., New York Times 2/14/06).

Purpose and Rationale

The question arises: does expression of trauma foster psychological health, or alternatively, does it interfere with recovery? Most likely neither of these recovery strategies is a blanket "best" approach for all survivors. Instead, each strategy may be effective for an individual at different times or for different traumas. This study seeks a more nuanced understanding; what are the roles of both avoidance and expression in recovery? Those who have personally experienced trauma and recovery can shed light on this question.

In the present study, women who were child survivors of the Holocaust were interviewed. For many in child survivors, the period following the Holocaust was characterized by decades of silence (Pennebaker, Barger, & Tiebout, 1989; Valent, 1995). Yet today, many choose to speak and find speaking out to be healing and fulfilling (Valent, 1995).

These women can shed light on the debate and help us to understand what makes disclosure possible and helpful. Additionally, by describing their experiences of silence or expression as related to psychological health, participants can inform the future study of traumatic sequelae and individual differences in the need for therapeutic interventions. In learning what survivors find beneficial in their recovery from childhood traumas, we may begin to understand what roles avoidance and expression play in coping and recovery. We may also gain a better understanding of the meaning of silence and voice in the face of trauma.

CHAPTER II

TRAUMA & COPING LITERATURE REVIEWS

The trauma section will review the definitions of trauma, define what is meant by "Hidden Children," and discuss the typical trauma sequelae of child survivors of the Holocaust. The coping section will explore resilience, coping and recovery in terms of both facing and turning away from the traumatic event through ecological and developmental frames.

Trauma Literature Review

Defining Trauma

The definition of trauma varies throughout the literature, as authors often fail to identify the differences between trauma, stressful events, crisis, psychological symptoms and reactions to traumatic events (Alpert, 2007; Dulmus & Hilarski, 2003; Weathers & Keane, 2007). It is helpful to understand trauma as three distinct components: (1) the environmental input (an event), (2) the individual's perception or appraisal of the event (the interaction of person and stressor), and (3) the psychological reactions of the individual (Green, 1990). Most discussions of trauma in the literature focus on one of these three aspects as centrally definitive (Davidson & Foa, 1991; Kilpatrick, 2005; Rechtman, 2004; Tennant, 2003; Thomas, 2004). In addition to these three definitive components, the diagnostic category of Post Traumatic Stress Disorder has been applied to clarify the term, and the diagnosis is a way to operationalize the concept of trauma (DSM-IV-TR, 2000). Given the variety of post-trauma reactions and symptoms (including the absence of any symptoms), however, practitioners and researchers have complained that the PTSD diagnosis does not comprehensively capture the repercussions of trauma (Cook et al., 2005; Courtois, 2008; Spinazzola et al., 2005).

Trauma as an Event

Trauma may refer to an event (the environmental input) that an individual experiences. This definition requires a universally recognized notion of what stressors are traumatizing to the victim (Weathers & Keane, 2007). However, regardless of the homogeneity of the stressors, individual interpretations and reactions to the same stressor vary (Axelrod, Grabowski, & Trewhella, 2007; Dulmus & Hilarski, 2003). The Diagnostic and Statistical Manual-IV enumerates a list of events, some of which are experienced directly, and others of which are merely witnessed or learned from experiences of others (DSM-IV-TR, 2000). The events in this list are often deemed "traumas" when adapted for measures in a variety of studies, despite the problematic variability in individual's responses to these events (for example, measures of exposure to trauma identified in Elhai, Gray, Kashdan, & Franklin, 2005). Some researchers have compensated for response variability by referring instead to a "potentially traumatic event" (PTE) which accounts for the fact that not all persons experience such an event as trauma (e.g., Bonanno & Mancini, 2008). In addition, stressful events are not of equal value. Nevertheless, the degree of severity of the stressors is not reflected as a continuum in this theoretical lens.

Trauma as Perception

Perceived trauma refers to the individual's personal appraisal and interpretation of the event. This definition is based on an interactionist theory positing that trauma lies in the interplay between the person and the stressor. The way an individual appraises a stressful event is unique for each person, even if the event is shared with others (Dulmus & Hilarski, 2003). According to this definition, the victim's subjective experience, understanding, and interpretation of the event is what constitutes trauma (Campbell, 1989). This definition may be problematic, however, as the subjective component widens the parameters or perhaps eliminates the parameters. An individual could potentially identify anything distressing as trauma (Davidson & Foa, 1991).

Trauma as a Psychological Reaction

The definition of trauma as a psychological reaction relies on the symptoms, or outcomes (response) of the individual (Green, 1990). If the individual exhibits signs common in traumatized populations, these signs are labeled traumas (Shahifar & Fox, 1997). This definition of trauma is closely linked to the diagnostic label of Post Traumatic Stress Disorder (PTSD). In order to merit this diagnosis, a direct link must exist between the event or stressor and the symptoms (DSM-IV-TR, 2000). This may be problematic, however, because the individual may not be able to link their outcomes to the event as the effects of the stressor may make that connection cognitively impossible for the individual (Breslau, Chase, & Anthony, 2002). Another potential problem with this definition lies in the circularity of the argument (a person has experienced trauma when she has been traumatized). Finally, a diagnosis of PTSD is limited as the definition of trauma, as the disorder is not the only outcome of exposure to traumatic stressors (Kilpatrick, 2005). Indeed, some traumatized individuals may not exhibit PTSD symptoms (Grand & Alpert, 1993), while others may exhibit posttrauma symptomotology for which the PTSD diagnosis is insufficient (Cook et al., 2005; Courtois, 2008; Spinazzola et al., 2005).

Definition of Trauma for the Purposes of This Study

For purposes of this study, one definition of trauma is not sufficient. The singularity of each survivor's experience and reaction nullifies the utility of one definition. In adhering to the first definition, trauma as an event, one could conclude that all survivors were traumatized merely because they endured the Holocaust. This definition fails to account for the variability in the individual survivor's interpretation of and reactions to the event. In adhering to the second definition, trauma as perception, variability is expected, and may be more relevant to the participant's experience. However, those survivors who exhibit strong resilience or repression could fail to meet this definition of trauma, claiming that although they endured a potentially traumatic event, they were not traumatized. The third definition, trauma as a psychological reaction, may not be useful here. Establishing the link between Holocaust events and the effects experienced decades later is difficult, given the fallibility of memory (although this investigator has no doubt about the historical veracity of the Holocaust) and the confounding individual experiences endured since. The focus of the present study is not on the events the victims endured; trauma is inferred. Rather, it is on how survivors view their own recovery from the Holocaust traumas they endured.

Trauma Survivors

Hidden Children: Who Are They?

The majority of living survivors of the Holocaust were infants, children, and adolescents at the time. Many individuals' developmental pathways to adulthood were forever changed by the traumatic effects of witnessing and enduring the Nazi attempt to exterminate their race. Some estimate that as many as 11% of Europe's prewar Jewish children survived the Holocaust (www.ushmm.org), while other accounts put the child survival rate at 7%. Both statistics are lower than the overall survival rate of all Jewish European adults and children, which is 33% (Tec, 1993). The majority of the child survivors were spared because they were hidden, having escaped to a hiding place or denied their identity and passed as Christian. Of these hidden children, most alternated between hiding and passing. The majority of those unable to hide or pass were either killed upon reaching concentration camps or died in the camps (retrieved from: //www.ushmm.org/museum/exhibit/online/ hiddenchildren; Tec, 1993). The term "Hidden Child" was originally coined at the 1991 the First International Gathering of Children Hidden During World War II. This summit was attended by child survivors of the Holocaust from more than 28 countries (retrieved from: //www.adl.org/hidden/ history.asp).

As Jewish parents became aware of the growing threat of the Nazi Regime, many hid their children in an attempt to save them from the horrors spreading across Europe. These children of the Holocaust were hidden in orphanages, convents, monasteries, in forests, with faraway relatives, and even with Christian strangers. Those children hidden by others were "passively hiding." Those who were not hidden in clandestine places assumed Christian identities and were "actively hiding." Many of the children were too young to remember life before the Holocaust or did not learn of their Jewish heritage until after the war (Tec, 1993).

Some passively hidden children remained concealed in enclosures such as attics, closets, caves, sewers, basements, and other confined areas. Often they were crammed into small spaces with other Jews. These concealed children are categorized as "invisible," and may have experienced different traumatic events than those children who were actively hiding. The invisible hidden children often lived in hunger and were under constant threat of being discovered. The visible (actively hidden) often bore witness to the horrors of daily life for Jews in their communities, including assassinations, beatings, rapes, and deportation to concentration camps (Fogelman, 1993). In addition, actively hidden children had to lead double lives as they masqueraded as Christians. Again, many children experienced hiding both visibly and invisibly, alternating between hiding and passing as the Holocaust unfolded over time (Tec, 1993).

While some hidden children initially entered hiding with a parent or parents, the parent did not always remain with the child, and many were found and killed or taken away to a camp. Others were separated from their families from the beginning of the Holocaust until after the liberation, when those parents who managed to survive concentration camps returned to reclaim their children. These reunions were rarely happy events (Bluglass, 2003; Tec, 1993). The child, if old enough to remember the parent, felt abandoned and angry. If not old enough, the child often resisted leaving foster parents or harboring families to accompany a stranger that claimed to be her parent. Often, the survivor's attempt at reconstructing a life was additionally traumatizing as he or she returned home to a changed world, and was met with anti-Semitism, abuse, and fear (Fogelman, 1993). Despite the variability in their experiences, hidden children shared basic features of suffering:

> Jewish children in hiding learned by necessity a host of survival strategies to cope with fears, imminence of death, starvation, freezing weather, illness, being invisible or maintaining a low profile, and loneliness. Most important was not to express any opinions or feelings and to remain silent (Fogelman, 1993, p. 295).

Regardless of the idiosyncratic suffering and variety of responses to potentially traumatic events, it is inferred from the literature on Holocaust experiences of hidden children that this population experienced multiple and repeated traumas.

Sequelae of Survivors who were Children during the Holocaust

Traumatic events and reactions to such events exist on a continuum. Over the past two decades, practitioners and researchers have recently been striving to capture the difference between milder traumatic reactions and those that are more severe than is reflected in the diagnosis of PTSD (Briere & Spinazzola, 2005; Herman, 1992; Terr, 1991). Two distinct trauma categories have emerged: simple traumas and complex traumas. Simple traumas result from the acute, isolated experience: "one sudden blow," whereas complex trauma reactions are: "the results of long-standing or repeated ordeals" (Terr, 1991, p.11). The experiences of the Hidden Children merit the latter category, which has been labeled "Complex Posttraumatic Stress Disorder" (CPTSD) (Glicksman & Van Haitsma, 2002).

This CPTSD label, was conceived of by Pelcovitz and colleagues (1997) as an addition to the DSM based on Judith Herman's (1992) concept of complex trauma. The label has most frequently been applied to victims of pervasive and complicated traumatic situations including, but not limited to, those engaged in armed combat, prisoners of war, displaced populations due to ethnic cleansing, refugees, those forced into human trafficking or prostitution, and those undergoing chronic medical problems (Cook et al., 2005; Courtois, 2008; Spinazzola et al., 2005).

CPTSD is most often associated with traumas that are interpersonal in nature (e.g., violence or war). A survey of metal health providers in the United States in 2002 revealed that the most prevalent form of complex trauma exposure for children fell under the category of interpersonal victimization. For this national study, the categories of trauma exposure in childhood meriting the CPTSD diagnosis, in order of prevalence, included: *Emotional Abuse, Loss, Impaired Caregiver, Domestic Violence, Sexual Abuse, Neglect, Physical Abuse, War/Terrorism (U.S.), Injury/Accident, Illness/Medical, Disaster, War/Terrorism (Int'l),* and *Forced Displacement* (Spinazzola et al., 2005). The trauma of hidden children falls within at least one, and in some cases, many of these categories (e.g., *Loss, War, Forced Displacement*, and in some cases *Impaired Caregiver, Abuse, Neglect*). Thus, CPTSD is most helpful in conceptualizing child survivor trauma.

While not officially recognized by the DSM-IV, a unifying set of criteria has been proposed and widely adopted for Complex PTSD that may better encompass the traumatic reactions of those who have been repeatedly exposed to multiple traumas (Courtois, 2008; Herman,1992). CPTSD is defined by six main symptom clusters: *altered self-capacities, cognitive disturbance, mood disturbance, overdeveloped avoidance responses, somatoform distress,* and *posstraumatic stress* (Briere and Spinazzola, 2005). These clusters most accurately address the child survivor's reported symptoms and will be framed here in the context of the Holocaust literature (Klein & Kogan, 1993).

The first cluster, *altered self-capacities*, refers to the "dysfunctions in the areas of identity, affect regulation, and interpersonal relatedness" (Briere and Spinazzola, 2005, p.402). Many child survivors suffer from distorted images of the self and a loss of cohesive identity, which may be the most "outstanding" psychological effect of enduring the Holocaust as a child (Amir & Lev-Wiesel, 2003, p.295). Certainly, identities of hidden children were affected, as their survival required the literal denial of a part of self for fear of extermination (Amir & Lev-Wiesel, 2001). In the case of the Holocaust survivor, the identity is negotiated in reaction to an unstable and eroded environment. In the Holocaust's "culture of terror," survivors experienced a diminished capacity for developing cohesive, authentic selves in relation to a fragmented context (Lewin, 1993, p.

310). In addition, interpersonal difficulties are oft-cited for survivors in terms of marital problems and family relationship troubles (Chodoff, 1997; Cohen, Dekel, Solomon, & Lavie, 2003; Dasberg, 2001; Laub & Auerhahn, 1989). A more comprehensive review of childhood trauma's impact on identity and coherence is found in the following section entitled *Trauma's Impact on Identity Development Over the Lifespan.*

The second cluster, *cognitive disturbance*, includes "low self-esteem, self-blame, helplessness, hopelessness, expectations of rejection and loss, and an over-determination of the amount of danger in the world" (Briere and Spinazzola, 2005, p.402). Many hidden children report "Survivor guilt": feelings of guilt and responsibility for being spared when hundreds of thousands of others died (Chodoff, 1997; Dasberg, 2001; Marks, 1993). Many survivors report confused and disoriented thought processes regarding their Holocaust experiences (Sagi, van IJzendoorn, Joels, & Scharf, 2002). Cognitive disturbances are likely compounded by the knowledge that the traumatic events of the Holocaust were not "acts of God," (natural disasters), but rather "of human design" (human-made traumatic events) (DSM-IV-TR, 2000, p. 463). This distinction is important in understanding the traumatization of Holocaust survivors; their interpersonal expectations are likely skewed due to first-hand knowledge of the horrors of human capacity.

The third cluster, *mood disturbance*, refers to symptoms "involving anxiety, depression, anger, and aggression" (Briere and Spinazzola, 2005, p.402). The prevalence of anxiety, anger, and depression in child survivors is well-documented (Kestenberg, 1980). Anger at abandoning parents and feelings of aggression were common in hidden children (Sagi, van IJzendoorn, Joels, & Scharf, 2002). Additionally, irrational fears and anxiety may have developed regarding triggers that created flashbacks to the trauma (Fogelman, 1993). When compared to their non-traumatized counterparts, child survivors routinely report higher levels of depression, anxiety, and anger-hostility, and they rate their psychological quality of life significantly lower (Amir & Lev-Wiesel, 2001; Amir & Lev-Wiesel, 2003; Chodoff, 1997; Sigal & Weinfeld, 2001).

Overdeveloped avoidance responses, the fourth cluster, refers to "overdevelopment of avoidance activities that appear to reduce the experience of trauma-related dysphoria" (Briere and Spinazzola, 2005, p.402). Avoidance reactions are evidenced in survivors, including reported techniques to dissociate from their Holocaust experiences, ranging from substance abuse to the avoidance of talking about their traumatic experiences with their children (Fogelman, 1993; Shmotkin, Blumstein, & Modan, 2003). Indeed, such avoidance responses are at the heart of this research, as many Holocaust survivors spent decades avoiding situations that would trigger trauma-related emotions or memories (Kidron, 2009).

The fifth cluster, *somatoform distress*, refers to "bodily distress or dysfunction" that results from the traumatic stressor (Briere and Spinazzola, 2005, p.403). Almost six decades after WWII, child survivors of the Holocaust rated their physical quality of life significantly lower and somatization (conversion of anxiety into physical symptoms) significantly higher than individuals who had not experienced the Holocaust (Amir & Lev-Wiesel, 2003). Similar reports abound of survivors' physical symptoms including ulcers, headaches, stomachaches, fatigue, listlessness, and inability to sleep (Amir & Lev-Weisel, 2001; Chodoff, 1997; Sigal & Weinfeld, 2001; Valent, 1995).

Finally, *posttraumatic stress* refers to the typical diagnostic criteria that include "intrusive re-experiencing," "avoidance," or "autonomic hyperarousal (e.g., heightened startle responses or insomnia)" (Briere & Spinazzola, 2005, p.403). Nearly every study conducted with Holocaust survivors includes a standard PTSD scale measuring symptom groups such as intrusion, avoidance, and arousal. Adult survivors who were children during the Holocaust repeatedly exhibit higher PTSD symptom scores than control populations (Amir & Lev-Wiesel, 2001; Amir & Lev-Wiesel, 2003; Barel et al., 2010; Chodoff, 1997; Cohen, Dekel, Solomon & Lavie, 2003; Sigal & Weinfeld, 2001; Valent, 1995).

Gender Differences in the Experience of Trauma

Gender plays a critical role in the investigation of trauma and recovery: it influences one's own understanding of trauma, it affects the way in which this trauma is related in narrative, and it has been shown to be a determining factor in the ways in which the individual copes with traumatic events and symptoms. The disproportionate diagnosis of PTSD in females has been repeatedly noted in the literature; by most accounts, PTSD rates among women are twice as high as men (Keane, Marshall, & Taft, 2006; Olff, Langeland, Draijer, & Gersons, 2007; Tolin & Foa, 2006). Traumatic events may trigger engendered responses to distress: one study found that compared to males, traumatized females endorsed more self-blame for the event, greater belief that they were incompetent or damaged, and greater belief that "the world is dangerous" (Tolin & Foa, 2006, p.980).

The potentially traumatic events each gender is likely to encounter differ, which may account for the different symptomotology. For example, one study conducted in war-torn Bosnia noted that males were more likely to endure the violence of combat (e.g., shooting and weapon-induced injury), while "women and girls reported more losses due to the war, maltreatment (sexual and physical abuse), and had relatives or close friends who had been wounded during war" (Gavranidou & Rosner, 2003, p.131). However, one study on the effects of Holocaust trauma discovered no gender differences were found in terms of reported trauma exposure, and PTSD symptoms were similar among males and females (Yehuda, Schmiedler, Siever, Binder-Brynes, & Elkin, 1997). For children, gender influenced exposure to trauma in the Holocaust. Male hidden children were especially susceptible to being "found out," as they bore the unique physical mark of their Jewish identity (circumcision). Therefore, male child survivors are relatively rare and were less successful at hiding (most were killed or sent to concentration camps) (Tec, 1993).

The recollection and report of traumatic events and symptomotology is likely to be influenced by gender, as traditional gender norms influence one's willingness to disclose. Also, certain traumas may be more likely to be endorsed by one gender over another (Gavranidou & Rosner, 2003). For example, men may be more reluctant to report sexual trauma (Tolin & Foa, 2006). Gender differences in those reports of trauma may also depend on the method of data collection;

questionnaires tend to largely favor incidents more likely to occur for males. Alternately, narrative methodologies may inherently influence individuals to conform to traditional social roles as well, encouraging, for example, women to present as more vulnerable and sensitive than their male counterparts (Gavranidou & Rosner, 2003).

Complex Trauma in Children

The developmental phase in which an individual endures complex trauma shapes the posttraumatic effects. Researchers and practitioners distinguish a number of factors that make complex trauma more challenging for children, including underdeveloped cognitive skills with which to make sense of the trauma, inability to separate reality from fantasy, relative inexperience in coping with stress, and reliance on adults who may also be compromised due to the trauma (Scheidlinger & Kahn, 2005; Williams, 2006). Complex trauma can result in a permanently changed sense of people, life, and the future, as these children are robbed of healthy optimism and protective naïveté (Terr, 1991).

Trauma impacts the child's developing brain and neurochemistry, and may also cause enduring memory problems (DeBellis, 1999). One study of CPTSD in children (Brennen et al., 2010) explains that if complex trauma interferes with memory development around age three or four, "normal development of retrieval of autobiographical memories will be prevented because growing up in such an environment would foster a tendency to avoid retrieval of specific memories to avoid negative affect" (p.241). Traumatic memories are thus encoded by the child in a disjointed way that prevents consolidation and is characterized by deadened emotion and blocked memory (Williams, 2006). Avoidance is employed to cope with the overwhelming nature of the events: complex trauma in children is frequently manifested in symptoms of denial, numbing, and dissociation. Dissociation may be a healthy response to a traumatic situation and may serve a child well initially, but may not serve her well at a later time (Terr, 1991).

Are the symptoms of child survivors the same as those of hidden children?

Studies investigating possible differences in the level of distress between groups who endured different traumatic Holocaust experiences (e.g., concentration camps, forced labor camps, ghettos, hiding) have found mixed results. One study (Shmotkin & Blumstein, 2003) found that while child survivors continued to endure traumatic after-effects and were worse off than non-traumatized controls, there were no differences in effects between those survivors who had been in concentration camps versus those who were not incarcerated. This finding, which duplicates results of other studies (e.g.,Yehuda et al., 1997), suggests that the cumulative effects of trauma may show decreasing variability with age, and child survivor symptoms may look similar across contexts. Survivors of complex trauma are believed by many to manifest similar symptoms, "independent of the causation situation" (Williams, 2006, p.322). Alternatively, one recent study found evidence that survivors in hiding exhibited more PTSD symptoms than those who had experienced concentration camp trauma. Hidden children exhibited particularly pervasive symptoms of avoidance and increased arousal compared to those who were in concentration camps (Prot, 2010).

Identity is an arena of divergence between the effects of trauma in hidden survivors versus those who had other Holocaust experiences. Hidden children experienced the unique trauma of having to deny their Jewish identities during the life phases in which identity development is crucial (Richman, 2006). Many have documented the unspeakability of the horrors of trauma, which, for hidden children, had an added layer of injunction against speaking (Lentin, 2000). For hidden children, to speak about themselves, their families, or their community would have meant mortal danger, thus they were mandated to remain silent (Gheith, 2007). The mandate to be quiet and deny one's identity permeated the culture for many Jews facing the Holocaust (Kidron, 2009; Schwartz, 2006).

Trauma's Impact on Identity Development over the Lifespan

Erik Erikson's theory of development provides a framework of understanding for both the suffering of child survivors and their efforts at coping with trauma. Erikson's theory focuses on identity; he explored identity as a central, lifelong quest characterized by an individual's striving toward self-acceptance in the context of a wider society (Miller, 2002). Identity is an important construct for survivors, as trauma violates one's conception of the self, and the goal of recovery is "to integrate and contextualize their experience within the existing mental representations of the self" (Dalgleish, Hauer, & Kuyken, 2008, p.259). Additionally, for hidden children, their denial of identity is central to their experience of trauma (Kidron, 2009).

While the lifespan consists of particular periods during which formation of the self is particularly salient, identity is a process of becoming throughout life as the individual negotiates through eight conflicts while seeking to avoid pain and to develop positive sense of oneself. According to Erikson, a positive and healthy identity lies in an accepted and fully integrated self (James & Zarrett, 2006). Unhealthy identity, on the other hand, is characterized by a lack of cohesion, which, in fact, is identified as a cardinal symptom of complex trauma and identified as "dissociation" (DSM-IV-TR, 2000). For hidden children, denial of one's identity hinders the development of cohesion, an added blow on top of the obliterating effects of the traumas survivors endured (Richman, 2006).

Identity, according to Erikson's psychosocial theory of development, evolves throughout the lifespan as the individual navigates multiple life crises, gaining *ego strengths* upon resolution of each crisis and ultimately attaining *ego integrity*. For Holocaust survivors, later life is Erikson's theorized time for integration and making peace with the past. Erikson's eighth stage of the life-cycle posits that these survivors are experiencing their final life "crisis": integrity versus despair, from which the construct of *wisdom* arises. Wisdom refers to the individual's achievement of integrative acceptance of the past, and without it, one may be regretful and remorseful about life. This is the final step of the eight stages. As the survivor reaches the end of life, the potential to actualize this strength of wisdom increases. One would therefore expect aging survivors to be pulled toward integrative reflection on their lives' experiences (Markstrom, Sabino, Turner, & Berman, 1997; Norman, McCluskey-Fawcett, & Ashcraft, 2002; Torges, Stewart, & Duncan, 2008).

According to Erikson's model, ego strength is epigenetic; each part has ascendancy that grows at its special time to become part of a gestalt. The eight ego strengths are present throughout the lifespan and undergo ascendance with the successful resolution of each stage. Therefore, ego strengths may provide evidence of psychosocial health both for each stage, and for overall strength and resiliency (Markstrom et al, 1997). Several factors are important for ascendance of the ego strength, rooted both in the individual's potential to resolve the conflict, and in the surrounding environment's social forces and conditions. Ego strength is likely to be affected by childhood trauma; without society's provisions, development and investment of the individual is compromised. For Holocaust children, the potential for ego strength at each stage of psychosocial development could be compromised by the traumatic effects of the Holocaust. If the Holocaust interfered with the successful resolution of even one stage, it is likely that subsequent crises might not be managed as well (Hoegh & Bourgeois, 2002). Indeed, evidence suggests that survivors have struggled inordinately with developmental crises. Typical symptoms of survivors will be presented here in the context of Erikson's theory.

With resolution of the first crisis in infancy, the ego strength of *hope* arises (trust and a feeling of certainty in life). Its antipathy, withdrawal, is based on doubt and faithlessness about life, others, oneself, and the future (Markstrom et al., 1997). This struggle is a theme in the literature of many Holocaust survivors, whose basic sense of security is disrupted (Amir & Lev-Wiesel, 2001). This ego strength of hope may be less developed in child survivors, many of whom were infants at the start of World War II.

Will is the ego strength growing from the second crisis, and is characterized by the awareness of and determination to apply free choice. Impotence, helplessness, and a lack of self-control may come from underdeveloped will, and is characterized by compulsivity and impulsivity. Indeed, survivors routinely report struggles with self-discipline and diminished feelings of dominance and assertiveness (Blum, 2007).

The third crisis' successful resolution gives rise to *purpose,* the courage to envisage and pursue valued goals. Its antithesis results in an aimless approach to life and a hesitancy to pursue goals. Holocaust survivors are less spontaneous and report lower levels of energy than non-traumatized controls (Nadler & Ben-Shushan, 1983).

Competence is the ego strength to freely use abilities and intelligence in tasks without fear of failure, and it arises in the crisis of school-aged children. Holocaust survivors often report feelings of worthlessness and inadequacy, which is indicative of an underdeveloped ego strength of competence (Shmotkin, Blumstein, & Baruch, 2003). For surviving hidden children, these first four crises would have occurred during the time in they endured the Holocaust, and would therefore be impacted by it.

Fidelity is perhaps Erikson's most studied ego strength, and much research has been generated around the adolescent psychosocial stage of identity vs. identity confusion (Adams & Montemayor, 1983). Adolescence marks the transition from childhood to adulthood, during which individuals struggle between commitment to truth and a genuine self, and the absence or defiance of self. This struggle is important within the context of the Holocaust; the survival of many Jewish adolescents required the literal denial of a part of self and identity for fear of extermination. In fact, research emphasizes this: "the most outstanding psychological effects of persecution are the loss of identity and feelings of being worthwhile" (Amir & Lev-Wiesel, 2003, p.295).

The remaining three ego strengths, *Love*, *Care*, and *Wisdom*, are central to adult development and are therefore not presumed to be achieved within the duration of the Holocaust for hidden children. However, given the epigenetic nature of ego strength, these three build on and may be influenced by the base of the previous five. In fact, Holocaust survivors frequently cite an impaired ability to achieve warm and trusting relationships with others (Nadler & Ben-Shushan, 1983). The unique suffering of hidden children may be most evidenced by compromised ego integrity and identity.

The goal of therapy, then, would presumably be to help the survivor achieve an evolved state of integration in order to reach the pinnacle of development- *ego integrity* (James & Zarrett, 2006). Indeed, studies indicate that a child survivor's sense of identity and ability to articulate a coherent sense of self in later life serves as a protective, moderating factor against posttraumatic symptoms (van der Hal-van Raalte, van IJzendoorn, & Bakermans-Kraenburg, 2008). Regardless of the particular stage of development a survivor might have been living through during the Holocaust, her individual ego strengths and ego integrity as a whole would be impacted. It follows, then, that therapy focused on identity and geared at increasing integration would be useful (Markstrom et al, 1997).

Feminine Perspective of Development

According to Erikson's theory of development, successful resolution of many of life's stages depends on the individual's increasing autonomy, inherently valuing the movement towards independence and separateness. Other theorists have argued, however, that his theory is far from universal; it accounts only for the developmental trajectory of males. Carol Gilligan's work points to the importance of relationship and connectedness for female identity: a "self in relationship." This gender difference is not accounted for by Erikson's theory (Gilligan,1982). Evidence presented by Dr. Gilligan and others (e.g., Strouse, 1974) merit a reworking of Erikson's theory to reflect the engendered experience of development that no longer values the masculine perspective over the feminine. Some call for such changes regarding particular stages (e.g., intimacy vs. identity; Horst, 1995), while others believe the insensitivity to gender differences renders Erikson's theory useless as it can "offer limited insight into the experiences and perspectives of those groups that have been excluded from the theory-building process and, in particular, cannot offer legitimate frameworks for research about women's lives or the lives of others from marginalized groups" (Sorell & Montgomery, 2009, p.98).

For female survivors of childhood trauma, disruption in relationships is likely to be uniquely damaging to a developing self. While Erikson's gender-biased model may not be the best gauge of psychological health for females, it nevertheless has utility as a general framework for conceptualizing developmental problems resulting from trauma.

Coping Literature Review

Resilience

Resilience refers to "the human capacity to thrive" in spite of experiencing traumatic events. It is a surprisingly common, though relatively under-investigated, phenomenon (Bonanno & Mancini, 2008). The concept of resilience is that individuals are able to maintain pre-trauma, baseline psychological health in the midst of exposure to severely disruptive trauma due to protective (salutogenic) factors (Mancini & Bonanno, 2009). As practitioners and researchers have begun to recognize that individuals can demonstrate remarkable resilience in the face of terrible trauma, many have concluded that an intervention is not required for everyone in order to return to pre-trauma levels of functioning and health (Litz, 2008). Resilience is a difficult construct to investigate for hidden children, as there is no way to currently, objectively measure their pre-trauma functioning, or to accurately account for personal characteristics which may have served as protective factors against their ensuing Holocaust experiences. Rather, this study's purpose is to investigate the coping strategies employed in the face of trauma (during exposure to potentially traumatizing events), as well as the recovery strategies that promoted the health of the hidden child (after exposure to potentially traumatizing events). Nevertheless, it is important to briefly review the literature regarding resilience, as it is an essential component of trauma that has bearing on the lives of the survivors, however immeasurable that impact may be.

Bonanno (2004) identifies *multiple pathways to resilience*, delineating individual characteristics that have proven protective against trauma. Some salutogenic factors include hardiness (which, in part, consists of the commitment to finding purpose in life and the belief that one can find benefit from hardship), self-enhancement (narcissism and high self-esteem), and positive emotion and laughter. Notably, these pathways are accessible to persons who possess these personal characteristics before they face trauma. Resilient individuals experience a continuity of identity; these are longstanding personality traits that are not simply adapted by individuals in the effort of coping post-trauma (Bonanno, Papa, & O'Neill, 2001). One of the key determinants of resilience, Mancini and Bonanno (2009) assert, is one's capacity to adapt behavior to meet stressors; this adaptability is rooted in pre-trauma, *a priori* beliefs and traits. For children, personality is just beginning to be formed; most hidden children did not have the benefit of having developed longstanding beliefs and traits (Williams, 2006).

Attachment dynamics with one's primary caregiver have also been linked to resilience. Much research has been conducted on Bowlby's (1980) work linking attachment to one's response to loss. While the nuanced findings will not be presented here, one finding consistently emerges: one's attachment style has an impact on resilience (for a more complete review, consult Mancini & Bonanno, 2009). In the healthy infant, the caregiver's responsive, flexible and adaptive attention promotes development of identity which sets the stage for a strong and stable sense of self that is likely to endure with continuity through trauma, protecting the child and buffering against the trauma (Jonsson, 2009). Of course, hidden children's attachment to their primary caregivers before the war varied, and this variability in attachment undoubtedly moderated the effects of the Holocaust. It is also important to consider that hidden children experienced disrupted attachments when separated from their parents. As young children, the stage of this disruption impacted the development of identity, compromising resilience (Prot, 2010; Williams, 2006).

This is not to say that hidden children did not exhibit resilience. Indeed, evidence abounds of many child survivors who were able to resume adaptive, productive, and healthy lives despite the trauma (e.g., Ayalon, 2005; Barel et al., 2010; Greene, 2002; Krystal, 2008; Sigal & Weinfeld, 2001). In one study of child survivors, van der Hal-van Raalte, van IJzendoorn, and Bakermans-Kranenburg (2008) identified a primary salutogenic factor that buffered against Holocaust trauma: sense of coherence. Sense of coherence regarding the potentially traumatic event refers to: (a) the ability to comprehend the event, (b) the ability to manage the situation, and (c) the ability to find meaning for the event. Multiple idiosyncratic factors determine one's ability to make coherent sense out of holocaust events, including intelligence, social support, family resources, and nature and degree of trauma, to name a few (Antonovsky, 1991). Again, one's developmental stage also impacts resilience; those who experienced the Holocaust as older children were better cognitively equipped to make coherent sense of what was happening. Nevertheless, one's ability to understand, control, and assign meaning to a potentially traumatic event limits the detrimental effects of that event on an individual.

Coping and Recovery

Resilience focuses on *prevention* of distress; effective coping and recovery styles are evidenced by the *alleviation* of emotional distress in an individual, permitting growth and thriving during and after a traumatic event (Brennan, Schutte, & Moos, 2006). Coping refers to how an individual adjusts during the traumatic event(s). Recovery refers to the individual's adjustment after the event(s). Mental processing styles vary among individuals during and after a traumatic event, and some styles may be more effective than others.

Two basic styles of psychological coping (during the event) exist for individuals enduring potentially traumatic events: 1) mindfully facing or 2) intentionally avoiding mentally processing the experience. Extensive literature exists for each coping style, yet the literatures are distinct and at odds, conceptualizing the styles as an either-or, "best choice" approach. Similarly, recovery (after the traumatic event) is divided into this same dichotomy: facing versus avoiding (Littleton, Horsley, John & Nelson, 2007). The terms facing down, integrating, processing, thinking about, and ruminating are used throughout to describe the process of "approach" behavior, and will herein be referred to as "expression." Expression in this context explains both the internal dialogue in which an individual may engage (one's expression of the quality and impact of the traumatic experience to oneself in one's own mind), and in the expression of the experience with others. This expression may not always take a narrative form, but may instead be non-narrative forms of approach behavior (Gheith, 2007). In contrast, behavior aimed at inhibiting, repressing, suppressing, ignoring, or refusing to focus on the traumatic experience is termed “avoidance.”

Expression as Effective

Psychotherapy, regardless of theoretical paradigm, is grounded in the notion of the healing power of talking about and “working through” trauma (Kidron, 2009). Basic to psychotherapy is the belief that in expressing and exploring the psychic impact of the trauma, one will become able to integrate the trauma into the existing mental schemata of the person, creating a cohesive self-narrative. In integration, conflicts are resolved, freeing the individual to cope effectively and recover (Bernsten & Rubin, 2007). Trauma expression is thought to help the individual gain a greater understanding of oneself. Insight and coherence is believed to encourage healthy coping and recovery from trauma (McLean, 2005). The healing effects of trauma expression, long-referred to as the “talking cure,” date back to Breuer and Freud’s cathartic model of the 1880’s (Herman, 1992). This assumption (talking leads to healing) underlies therapeutic efforts today, regardless of practitioner orientation (Bonanno, 2004; Bonanno, Keltner, Holen, & Horowitz, 1995; Cook, Spinazzola, Ford, et al., 2005; Herman, 1992; McNally, Bryant, & Ehlers, 2003; Miller, 2002; Rime, 1995; Zech & Rime, 2005).

Practitioners encourage the telling of traumatic narratives, and many believe that the telling of a cohesive story leads to posttraumatic growth (McNally, Bryant, & Ehlers, 2003; Meichenbaum, 2006; Neimeyer, 2006).

Narratives of one's life experiences and memories have been demonstrated to help individuals assign meaning to their lives, clarifying and solidifying identities, which promotes integrity (Haber, 2006; Phoenix, Smith, & Sparkes, 2010; Torges, Stewart & Duncan, 2009). The empirically supported therapeutic value of narrative disclosure has led to a burgeoning field called "narrative medicine," whereby medical professionals are trained to help their patients tell the story of their illnesses (Charon, 2001). Emotionally-charged narrative disclosure of patients has been shown to improve pain and well-being (Cepada et al., 2008; Harter & Bochner, 2009).

Interventions for traumatized individuals are often similarly geared at self-disclosure regarding one's experience, often in the hopes of creating a cohesive narrative. For children suffering from complex trauma, the empirically-supported "best practice" involves the integration of traumatic experiences, often through trauma-focused narration (Cohen & Mannarino, 2008; Ford, 2010; Ford, & Cloitre, 2009). The telling of one's experience is widely thought to be therapeutic for children, as evidenced by the implementation of a vast array of groups aimed at self-disclosure: crisis intervention groups, bereavement groups, groups for children of alcoholic families, groups for medically-ill children, trauma groups, etc. (Scheidlinger & Kahn, 2005). Indeed, talk therapy groups have been shown to foster an improved sense of mental coherence, (Langeland et al., 2006). The telling of one's narrative, evidence suggests, improves mental health and reduces anxiety and depression (Smyth, Hockemeyer, & Tulloch, 2008).

Trauma researchers argue that “in order to be successful, treatment for PTSD should facilitate the organization of the trauma narrative” (Feeny & Foa, 2006, p.293). Oral or written disclosure, debriefing sessions, and social sharing (an in-depth verbalization of the traumatic experience to another), have all been demonstrated to provide perceived benefits and emotional relief to victims (Rime, 1995; Zech & Rime, 2005). Given the mature age of remaining Holocaust survivors, the cohesive narrative and meaning-making of expression may be particularly relevant (Cassel & Suedfeld, 2006).

Those providing evidence in favor of expression often denounce avoidance as a maladaptive strategy for, and often a symptom of, ineffective coping. Kidron (2009) offers an assessment of the pervasive repudiation of avoidance in the field of psychology: "the absence of voice is understood as signaling psychopathologized processes of avoidance and repression, socially suspect processes of personal secrecy, or collective processes of political subjugation” (p.5). Pervasive, ongoing silence and avoidance are routinely characterized as pathological responses to trauma (Littleton, Horsley, John, & Nelson, 2007). Indeed, avoidance is at the heart of the definition of trauma pathology, formally labeled PTSD. The DSM-IV specifies avoidance as a very criterion of the disorder: “The person commonly makes deliberate efforts to avoid thoughts, feelings, or conversations about the traumatic event (Criterion C1) and to avoid activities, situations, or people who arouse recollections of it (Criterion C2)” (DSM-IV-TR, 2000, p. 464). The logic seems to be that if avoidance is pathological, expression is healthy.

Studies abound suggesting that individuals relying on avoidant coping styles suffer inordinately compared to those who rely on expression to cope. One study indicates that those who choose avoidance endorse greater daily negative affect and social anxiety and report less positive experiences and an overall diminished satisfaction with life compared to less-avoidant traumatized people (Kashdan, Barrios, Forsyth and Steger, 2006). Another study demonstrates that experiential avoidance (efforts to alter or avoid negative memories and situations that trigger memories) predicts dysfunctional outcomes and exacerbates anxiety (Kashdan, Breen, Afram, & Terhar, 2010). Thought suppression (keeping unwanted thoughts at bay), emotion suppression (trying to ignore and avoid expression of affect), and avoidant coping strategies have been linked to PTSD, anxiety, and depressive symptoms in both traumatized and non-traumatized populations (Amstadter & Vernon, 2008). Avoidance coping (as characterized in one study by denial, minimization, and avoidance of stressful experiences) apparently has lasting effects; avoidant style predicted chronic and acute stressors up to ten years later (Holahan, Moos, Holahan, Brennan & Shutte, 2005).

The mechanism of avoidance may be problematic for coping for several – somewhat paradoxical- reasons. As the avoidant individual turns her attention away from relevant threats, she may ignore or discount the detrimental effects of the threat. Such avoidant behavior, in turn, could paradoxically compromise her health (Schwerdtfeger, Schmuckle, & Egloff, 2006). Additionally, some researchers have documented what they call the "ironic effect" of effortful avoidance of negative emotion in the face of trauma. One study demonstrated that when individuals are under mental stress, efforts to "suppress any emotions that they felt" about a distressing autobiographical memory resulted, ironically, in greater increase of negative emotion (Dalgeish, Yiend, Schwizer, & Dunn, 2009, p.745). Efforts to avoid negative emotion have similarly been demonstrated to exacerbate posttraumatic symptoms (Dalgleish, Hauer, & Kuyken, 2008).

Avoidance as Effective

While largely pathologized, avoidance has also been associated with positive outcomes for traumatized populations. Avoidance has been conceptualized in the literature in a variety of ways from thought and emotion suppression, to silence, to effortful avoidance or alteration of memory. One study describes a three-part conceptualization of avoidance: avoidant coping (strategic attempts to escape stress), detached coping (becoming independent from aversive events and emotions) and the inhibition of emotional expression (Kashdan, Barrios, Forsyth and Steger, 2006). Each component has been empirically tied to positive outcomes. For heart attack victims, those patients who avoided threat-related aspects of the incident had lower stress symptoms than those who did not, suggesting that avoiding could buffer the stress of a traumatic experience (Ginzburg, Solomon, & Bleich, 2002).

The concept of inhibition of emotional expression has been the most studied component of avoidance and has elsewhere been labeled "emotional suppression" (Dalgleish, Hauer, & Kuyken, 2008) and "repressive coping" (Derakshan & Eysenck, 1997). Purported outcomes of this coping style vary. Contrary to evidence suggesting the paradoxical effects of avoiding distressing feelings, one study asserts that efforts to inhibit negative memories actually is effective at limiting negative mood (Geraerts, Hauer, Wessel, 2010). Inhibition of emotion can not only be an effective way of regulating affect, one study suggests, but is also associated with psychological health, fewer somatic complaints and health problems, and overall better adjustment compared to those who tend to adopt a more expressive coping style (Coifman, Bonanno, Ray, & Gross, 2007). Multiple studies suggest similar benefits of emotional inhibition: for bereaved spouses, emotional avoidance was associated with minimal grief and reduced somatic complaints up to 14 months after the death of their spouses (Bonanno, Keltner, Holen, & Horowitz, 1995).

In many studies, empirical evidence supports the initial beneficial effects of avoidance immediately following the traumatic event (e.g., Dalgleish, Hauer, & Kuyken, 2008; Littleton, Horsley, John, & Nelson, 2007). However, long-term effects of this coping style are less clear. Perhaps avoidance is effective in the initial period following a potentially traumatic event, but becomes detrimental over time. The victim's allocation of resources is likely to fluctuate over time, which allows for the adaptation of various coping styles (Baltes, Lindberger, & Staudinger, 1998).

Just as those in favor of expression denounce avoidance, researchers delineating the benefits of avoidance are skeptical of expression as the sole path to recovery. Spiro, Shalev, Solomon and Kotler (1989) report that a treatment program for war veterans suffering from PTSD that focused on the expression of traumatic experiences resulted in increased symptoms and diminished social functioning after the intervention. Expression following trauma can be harmful for children as well. Following September 11, 2001, more than 9000 therapists entered New York City schools in an attempt to minimize children's potential psychological damage from enduring this traumatic event. However, for students not suffering at the time from posttraumatic stress, this intervention impeded recovery (Gist & Devilly, 2002).

One meta-analytic review of the debriefing literature suggests that crisis interventions which encourage individuals to talk about their traumatic experiences have no positive benefits for the victims, and, in fact, may be upsetting (McNally, Bryant, & Ehlers, 2003). For some, therapeutic techniques aimed at processing post-trauma emotions (i.e., rehearsal or diary writing) may result in poorer recovery (Rime, 1995). Debriefing is still widely employed, and the treatment of traumatized individuals relies on the expression, processing, and talking through of potentially traumatic experiences (e.g., Cook, Spinazzola, Ford, Lanktree, et al., 2005). This trend toward processing and expression may be shifting in light of more recent research on the harmful effects of expression: trauma experts have begun to caution against the wholesale application of interventions aimed at expression of trauma, noting the harmful effects (e.g., Courtois, 2008; Ford, 2010).

Trauma treatment, as was previously mentioned, is often geared toward helping the victim create a cohesive narrative about their experiences. The incorporation of the trauma into an individual's life story, however, could be detrimental to one's well-being. One study demonstrates that when aversive, shameful emotional events become central in one's autobiographical narrative, one is more likely to experience depression and PTSD symptoms (Robinaugh & McNally, 2010). Similarly, the enhanced integration of a traumatic memory into one's life story (when it forms a reference point for the organization of other memories) is a predictor of PTSD symptoms, regardless of the degree of trauma severity (Bernsten & Rubin, 2007). This research suggests that the more central the trauma is to an individual's identity, the more distress one will experience. Therefore, talking about trauma in an effort to integrate it could be ill-advised.

While some evidence indicates that processing the event in the aftermath of trauma may not be beneficial to an individual's psychological health, many traumatized people nonetheless believe disclosing to others is helpful. In one study on benefits of social sharing (talking about an experience with another), individuals who shared an emotional memory perceived benefits from the exercise, and subjectively reported relief and greater insight after having shared. Despite this claim, perceived benefits were unrelated to recovery outcomes from participants' self-report symptom scales. While they said they felt better, symptom measures failed to reflect their assertions (Zech & Rime, 2005). This seemingly paradoxical evidence reinforces the need for a nuanced understanding of the intricate ways in which traumatized individuals view their own coping and recovery. This also highlights the need for research beyond quantitative, symptom scale methods in order to capture a complex story.

A Developmental & Ecological Context Outlook on Coping

Context and time frame are important considerations when investigating coping strategies of traumatized populations. During the Holocaust, the lives of hidden children literally depended on the ability to keep quiet and to silence their voices (Lentin, 2000; Schwartz, 2006). While silence characterized many survivors' coping strategies, it is qualitatively different than avoidance as described in trauma literature (e.g., Ginzburg, Solomon, & Bleich, 2002). Literature on Holocaust survivors suggests that avoidance, not just silence, was a common coping mechanism during, and following, traumatic experiences. Avoidance regarding the Holocaust was likely a result of the survivors' needs to forget past lives and identities in order to survive (Klein & Kogan, 1989). Avoidance strategies such as denial enabled individuals to withdraw emotionally and maintain hope during the Holocaust (Davidson, 1989).

Viktor Frankl (1992), a concentration camp survivor and eminent psychologist, highlights the possibility of growth from denying the mortifying reality of a traumatic situation. Frankl believed that a focus on the transcendent will to live and greater meaning for life is more adaptive than an attention to the horrors of reality during a traumatic event like the Holocaust. This coping strategy may foster healthier recovery after the trauma. According to Kaminer and Lavie (1993), those Holocaust survivors who were most well-adjusted evidenced "low penetration of traumatic memories, avoidance, and distancing from threatening stimulus, and repression of emotions" (cited in Bonanno, Keltner, Holen, & Horowitz, 1995, p.984).

Avoidance strategies have been demonstrated in children exposed to a range of complex traumas. One study of traumatized children asserts that the coping strategy children most frequently employ is to "inhibit the capacity to think, to feel, and to make links between intentions of others and their behavior. This means that they defensively numb themselves to the nuances of the outer world" (Fritsch, 2006, p.303). In one study of Holocaust survivors, hidden children demonstrated a higher degree of avoidance than other survivors (Prot, 2010). Avoidance as a defense may take different forms. For child survivors, avoidance has been noted in the form of fantasy formation (i.e., daydreaming); by means of distracting words (i.e. singing and praying); or action (i.e. playing); each strategy is thought to serve as a distraction from the traumatic situations of the Holocaust (Klein & Kogan, 1989).

In one study of family coping styles of Jewish families during the Holocaust, researchers discovered styles ranging from strict denial and avoidance of the topic to a depressed immersion in the trauma (Klein & Kogan, 1989). The heterogeneity in the range of responses of Holocaust survivors indicates that there is wide variability in the degree to which Holocaust survivors dealt with trauma and recovery (Chaitin, 2005). Most survivors, however, spent a long period of time avoiding the integration of their experiences, before shifting towards expression. One study (Pennebaker, Barger, & Tiebout, 1989) approximates that in 1985 only 30% of Holocaust survivors living in the United States had ever talked about their experiences. However, decades after the Holocaust, survivors began to share their stories, indicating a breakdown of denial (Davidson, 1989).

Avoidance strategies that were initially effective in the face of trauma evidently become maladaptive over the long run (Littleton, Horsley, John, & Nelson, 2007).

Again we return to developmental theory to help explain the shift from avoidance to expression. Successful aging, according to Erikson's theory, ultimately results in *ego integrity*, the culmination of eight ego strengths reflected in one's complex and holistic sense of integrated self (Torges, Stewart, & Duncan, 2008). Integrity results in part from life's stage of generativity, a time during which individuals reflect on their lives and turn their interest toward the future: leaving a legacy, giving to the next generation, and improving society. Indeed, one study examining narrative themes in aging female survivors' Holocaust testimony discovered that "belief in the historical importance of the Holocaust, the need to make meaning of the past, and encouragement from others emerged as important reasons for participants' willingness to disclose, in spite of reports that disclosure brought distress" (Finkelstein & Levy, 2006, p.117). These themes embody the notion of generativity.

Generativity in aging women has been integrally linked to a sense of identity, and is correlated with personality traits of self-esteem and expressiveness ((Norman, McCluskey-Fawcett, & Ashcraft, 2002). One longitudinal study of women (James & Zarrett, 2006) links midlife identity to later life generativity, leading the authors to conclude that "women who have a clear sense of themselves in young adulthood and who find avenues for expressing that self and identity, are able to meet later challenges (crises) more adroitly" (p.72). Given the challenges hidden children faced in expressing themselves, do they experience the period of generativity differently? Are hidden children similarly drawn towards self-expression in older age? Indeed, data indicates that in later life, many survivors move from avoidance to expression, and find speaking out to be healing and fulfilling (Lewin, 1993; Prot, 2010; Valent, 1995). For aging adults, finding meaning in the narrative of one's life has been demonstrated to buffer stress and offset trauma (Krause, 2007).

Survivors' strategies of recovery from trauma have changed from silence to speaking after a forty-year latency following the Holocaust (Valent, 1995). With the documented loss of personal and cultural resources due to the Holocaust, young survivors' goals were likely aimed at generating new resources. They may have needed to enlist trauma-avoidant strategies to begin rebuilding their lives (Baltes, Lindberger, & Staudinger, 1998). However, with time and age, these survivors may be pulled toward integrating their life experiences. In so doing, they can allocate resources to the preservation and legacy of their Holocaust experience and bear witness through their life stories (Valent, 1995). Evidence suggests that as individuals age, their coping styles change from eluding problems to taking direct action and employing problem-solving strategies (De Minzi & Sacchi, 2005). For Holocaust survivors, autobiographical disclosure has been encouraged and sanctioned through the public's interest in hearing their stories, further promoting speaking and integrating their life's history (Cassel & Suedfeld, 2006).

Studies on aging reveal that one's tendency to reminisce and create a life narrative increase as one grows older (e.g., Haber, 2006; Torges, Stewart, &

Duncan, 2009). As normal aging carries traumas such as illness and isolation and as the individual approaches death, it may be reminiscent of other traumatic memories and may trigger an individual to think more about past traumas. This is in line with life's eighth stage, where individuals in traumatized populations are reminiscing and struggling to integrate or revise the memory of the trauma, with waning time to do so (Prot, 2010).

Life Span Theory

Ecological context is essential to the understanding of response to trauma and post-trauma coping strategies (Hughes, Humphrey & Weaver, 2005). Indeed, "whether particular defenses are adaptive or maladaptive depends on the context and time frame in which they are used" (Olff, Langeland, Draijer, & Gersons, 2007, p.190). Life Span Theory provides a helpful framework to consider context in the debate of expression vs. avoidance, as it generates hypotheses about the transition from silence to speaking with regard to survivors. Life Span is a meta-theory that lends itself to the incorporation of developmental and contextual considerations across the span of one's life (Boerner & Jopp, 2007). The theory provides an explanation of why individuals leverage different coping strategies at different times in order to promote optimal development. According to the theory, optimal development relies on three major adaptive tasks in life: growth, maintenance, and/or regulation of loss. Depending on one's developmental phase or situation, one of these three tasks will be central to development (Baltes et al, 1998).

At the heart of Life Span Theory lies a model Baltes and his colleagues (1998) term the "SOC model." This model describes the mechanism by which an individual successfully develops. One employs three processes: selection (of a goal), optimization (means toward reaching goal), and compensation (regulation and compensation for loss in reaching goal). Each process works with the other two, coming together in different ways depending on the interaction of the individual, context, and time (Boerner & Jopp, 2007).

The SOC model suggests that individual's selection of a goal is either: (a) elective (whereby the individual chooses a goal) or (b) loss-based (whereby the individual's circumstance of loss mandates selection of a goal), depending on one's circumstances. For survivors, trauma presumably creates a situation in which goals are chosen in the face of loss, due to the "current unavailability of previously existing resources and from the limitations in resources" (Baltes, Lindenberger, & Staudinger, 1998, p.1056). With the documented loss of personal resources due to the Holocaust, one would choose goals and employ optimization strategies aimed at generation of new resources and reevaluation of goals to begin rebuilding their lives (Baltes et al, 1998).

According to the SOC model, childhood and adolescence's resources are allocated primarily toward growth. Today's survivors (who were children during the Holocaust) likely employed selection and optimization strategies (whether consciously or unconsciously) geared at growth and building resources following their trauma and loss. According to the principles of Life Span Theory, adolescent and early adult years would therefore not be the appropriate time developmentally to work through trauma, but rather to build a new identity and "move on" (Boerner & Jopp, 2007).

Successful aging, however, begins to require a different allocation to adaptive tasks, increasingly stressing maintenance, recovery, and the regulation of loss. With old age, the theory posits, dependency on others becomes salient and "the productive and creative use of dependency becomes critical" (Baltes et al., 1998, p. 1041). Sharing the burden of the trauma through interpersonal interaction and "talking through" to gain therapeutic support may become part of the individual's adaptive capacity, increasing or freeing up diminishing resources for efficacy. There is a shift in strategy to maximize growth; what may have been maladaptive in childhood is now necessary in old age. This shift in tasks is now appropriate for development: "a given developmental outcome achieved through SOC can at a [different] ontogenetic time or in a different context be judged as dysfunctional" (Baltes et al., 1998, p.1054). A new pathway to coping, which previously was not central or perhaps even detrimental for the individual, now serves to regulate loss.

Life Span's expansive focus on development as a lifelong process (even into old age) emphasizes the importance of continuing efforts to heal and understand survivors' experiences (Boerner & Jopp, 2007). The theory's notion that individuals are influenced by both biology and environment lends itself well to the study of trauma. The acknowledgement of both historical and idiosyncratic influences is particularly pertinent when dealing with a traumatized population in which each individual experienced her own unique set of traumas within the historical context of the Holocaust (Baltes et al., 1998).

While Erikson's theory suggests that healthy development over the lifespan involves integration of the self and cohesion, Life Span offers a more nuanced view of developmental health: "selectively attending to positive aspects of the self at different points in the lifetime [which] can serve to support a positive sense of self at the present" (Baltes et al., 1998, p1109). This selective attention inherent in Life Span Theory is termed *plasticity*, which refers to the flexibility and idiosyncratic nature of identity development. Indeed, developmental health in older women has been empirically defined in terms of plasticity: "having multiple sources of identity promotes positive aging" (Norman, McCluskey-Fawcett, & Ashcraft, 2002, p. 39). Flexible attention to one's history promotes healthy identity and aging: "As a given pathway of ontogenetic development is chosen and optimized, others are ignored or suppressed" (Baltes et al., 1998, p1045). This notion of plasticity is mirrored in studies on effective coping with trauma. *Emotional flexibility* is a term referring to one's adaptive ability to express or suppress emotion in accordance with situational demands, and has been identified as key in better self-reported adjustment following trauma (Westphal, Seivert, & Bonanno, 2010).

This plasticity or flexibility in optimal development sheds light on why some individuals find talking post-trauma therapeutic at times, while at other times they may find it detrimental. Perhaps repressing trauma can be adaptive immediately after the trauma as other elements of one's identity are more salient, but as one is pulled towards integration and the allocation of resources shifts as a function of healthy development, it can become detrimental. Additionally, the sociocultural context may determine others' willingness to listen to survivors and address the horrors of the Holocaust. The Zeitgeist can impact the pathway from silence to speaking.

Given the complex trauma that hidden children experienced and the many decades they have navigated coping with and recovering from the Holocaust, these survivors can serve as experts to inform the debate of expression versus avoidance. What can they tell us about their own pathways from silence to speaking? This study will not query those survivors who choose to remain silent about their Holocaust experiences. Indeed, those that remain silent may provide the richest information about the possible benefits of avoidance. However, those survivors who agree to share their narratives of coping and recovery have likely endured some period of silence before speaking. They may therefore be able to speak to both the pros and cons of silence and what later prompted them to share their Holocaust experiences with others. In addition, the variability in their experiences will add to the nuances in the pathways from silence to speaking. Their experiences with both styles may help inform the treatment of traumatized populations.

CHAPTER III

METHODOLOGY

Introduction

This chapter will review epistemological stance, methodology, criteria used for selecting participants for the study, procedures and methods, the data analysis plan, and evaluation criteria for this study. Ethical considerations will also be reviewed.

Epistemological Assumptions

The notion of triangulation is relevant to the ontological stance of the researcher. The individual perspectives of hidden children of the Holocaust shed light on the debate in trauma recovery literature. For this study, the two sides of the debate in the field (expression aids recovery from trauma vs. avoidance aids recovery from trauma) serve as additional perspectives in order to understand recovery from trauma and create the opportunity to engage in theory triangulation (Denzin, 1978). In collecting individual perspectives, this study encounters the dissonant or divergent data presented by the two theoretical camps. This leads to new understandings and a crystallized view of the complex picture of coping and recovery (Perlesz & Lindsay, 2003). Rather than operating from the positivist framework that one of the camp's evidence or argument more accurately captures the "correct" answer, this study seeks to discover a new, unique, and nuanced understanding of the survivor's experience of coping and recovery. In adding each survivor's perspective to these two theories, a richer picture of recovery from trauma can be ascertained.

Setting and Participants

Participants were recruited through the Hidden Child Foundation. The Hidden Child Foundation, an organization of the Braun Holocaust Institute of the Anti-Defamation League, was formed after an international gathering of child survivors of the Holocaust in 1991 (retrieved from://www.adl.org/hidden). The New York City chapter operates as the world headquarters of the foundation. An administrator of the Hidden Child Foundation, who is herself a Hidden Child and who has frequent contact with and access to the foundation's population, provided a letter of support for the study (see Appendix). The principal investigator provided the administrator with protocol on recruitment and screening using materials found in the Appendix. The administrator disseminated flyers and information to the membership body of the foundation. Additionally, the administrator notified hidden children through word-of-mouth. Interested candidates were screened by the recruiter according to the inclusion criteria questionnaire. The phone numbers of eligible candidates were then given to the Principal Investigator (PI) by the administrator. The PI met with each eligible candidate, introducing the study and obtaining consent before commencing a 60-180 minute interview. Participants were given the option to meet at their homes or at the headquarters of the Hidden Child Foundation. Further details on the procedure of this study are provided in the section entitled "Procedures."

Eight participants were recruited and interviewed for this project; six interviews were selected for inclusion in the study based on several factors. This study employed *purposeful sampling*, a procedure whereby individuals were successively interviewed until redundancy began to occur in the narrative content relevant to the research question (a concept termed *theoretical saturation*) (Lincoln & Guba, 1985). Redundancy in the content and themes related to coping and recovery was increasingly noted by the fifth interview. The PI, however, continued through eight interviews to ensure that enough interviews were available to provide theoretical saturation (Strauss & Corbin, 1998). *Theoretical saturation* refers to the notion that the researcher stops collecting interviews only when a category is clearly defined or exhausted. This notion mirrors Lincoln & Guba's (1985) notion of informational redundancy, distinguished by the procedure that one may stop interviewing when one determines that no new information is forthcoming. As the PI successively collected interviews, common themes began to emerge and each participant's ideas were reiterated by the next. Of course, each individual had a unique experience of trauma and healing, but the investigator determined that there were unified instances in six interviews that hung together as a cohesive, larger whole. It was determined that the remaining two interviews did not contain material that reiterated the emerging themes and unifying instances. While the transcripts from these interviews were sent to the participants for review, they were not included in the final analysis and results.

Participant Demographics

Name	Age at Hiding	Method of Hiding	Location	Age at Interview
Sonia	1 yo-toddler	Passing as Catholic; hiding father in home	Ukraine	66 yo
Anita	10 yo - teen	Hidden in a barn	Poland	78 yo
Connie	11 yo – teen	Hidden with a Christian family	Holland	79 yo
Fran	6 yo - preteen	Convent orphanage; passing as Christian; foster child of Christian families	France	73 yo
Reva	4yo – 5yo	Hidden in forest under care of forest watchman	Poland	72 yo
Yvonne	10yo-14yo	Hidden in convent	France	79 yo

In this study, only females were asked to participate. The reasoning behind this selection is both practical and theoretical. First, gender is a category of experience. The purpose of the study is to seek a crystallized, nuanced view of an experience. Therefore, by listening to the uniquely feminine experience, one may be able to go more deeply into the material without the confounding variable of gender that one might encounter if men were also interviewed. Practically, female participants were more easily accessible than males. This accessibility is related to two factors. The first is that male hidden children were especially susceptible to being "found out," as they bore the unique physical mark of their Jewish identity (a circumcised penis). Therefore, male child survivors are relatively rare and were less successful at hiding (Tec, 1993). The second is that the Hidden Child Foundation's New York chapter (a support group for child survivors from which the study recruited participants) is comprised of fewer males than females (according to the administrator). The number of participants in this study is consistent with other studies that have utilized the Listening Guide method and is estimated to provide reasonable power for qualitative narrative analysis when the goal is to capture the individual's Holocaust coping and recovery experience (Sandelowski, 1995).

Method

To meet the goals of this project, purposeful sampling from the Hidden Child Foundation's New York City chapter was employed. Semi-structured interviews were conducted by the PI with eight female participants (from which six were selected for this study). Each interview lasted an average of 120 minutes. The interviews were transcribed, sent to the participants for member checking (described below), and then qualitatively analyzed according to the Listening Guide. The researcher's epistemological stance that subjectivity neither can nor should be avoided in research is appropriately captured in the Listening Guide technique-a voice-centered, relational method by which this data was analyzed.

With respect to the current study's research questions, the methodology allowed for an exploration of the survivor's use of expression and avoidance in coping and recovery from trauma. Reports of coping strategies were allowed to emerge spontaneously throughout the course of the interviews, allowing for a rich, naturalistic glimpse of the interviewee's subjective experience. The questions in the semi-structured interview protocol were designed to address both sides of the debate in the literature (expression vs. avoidance), while permitting space for unanticipated findings and causal explanations to arise (Maxwell, 1996).

Procedures

The administrator of the Hidden Child Foundation served as the referral source, recruiter and screener of potential participants for this study. Participants were recruited via the investigator's scripts and flyers, as well as by word-of-mouth. They were screened according to the inclusion criteria below (and documented in forms found in the Appendix). Once included, participants were referred via telephone to the investigator, who then telephoned the participant directly to set up a face-to-face interview. Interviews were conducted by a Caucasian female interviewer (the present investigator), and were carried out either in the homes of interviewees or the Hidden Child Foundation's headquarters (the participant chose the location according to her preference). The investigator established rapport initially over the telephone via a formal introduction to the study, and again by an introduction during the first twenty minutes of the face-to-face meeting. *Figure 1* below provides a detailed account of the procedures used for this study.

Member Checking

The interview transcript was mailed to each of the original eight participants within three months of the date the interview was conducted, anchoring the evidence and permitting feedback to further ensure validity—a reflection of the co-construction between the investigator and the participant. The investigator enclosed a second consent form with the transcript, along with a stamped envelope addressed to the investigator. Participants were instructed to provide any edits to the transcript in writing and return them along with the second consent form, indicating that the use of their transcript was permitted. This process, known as "member checking," is considered by qualitative researchers to be "the most crucial technique for establishing credibility" (Lincoln & Guba, 1985, p.314). In line with the member checking process, the investigator edited the transcript as requested by the member (only one participant requested edits).

The present study focused on participants' responses to the following basic line of inquiry: "Some people who have experienced trauma such as the Holocaust find talking about it helpful and necessary, while others don't like to discuss it. How do you approach it?"and to accompanying probes. A semi-structured interview protocol guided the interviews. Interviewees were asked about their recovery styles and strategies for coping since the time of the Holocaust. The focus was on expression or avoidance of the trauma (the list of probes can be found in the Appendix). The interviewer's use of probes depended on the content of a participant's particular response, the need for clarification or for encouraging the participant to expand upon her answer. Variation was expected and occurred in the order in which questions and probes were asked. The effort was always to preserve the natural flow of the dialogue. All interviews were audio-taped by a digital recorder and subsequently transcribed. The verbatim transcripts were used as the sources for content analyses. Digital files of the recording were labeled only with a letter, which was recorded on participants' consent forms. These forms were kept along with the recorder in the author's locked files. When requested by the participant, transcripts were stripped of identifying information. Transcripts were kept on the hard drive of a password-protected computer. None of the participants accepted the offer of destruction of the original audio-taped data.

Flow Chart of Procedures

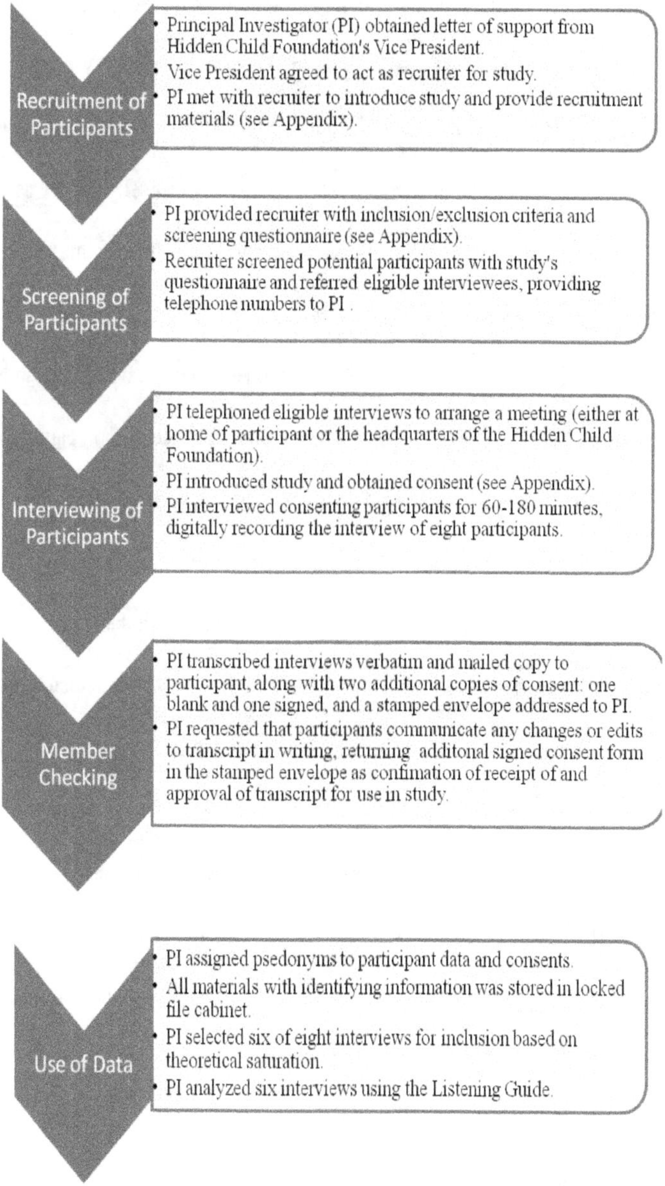

Recruitment of Participants

- Principal Investigator (PI) obtained letter of support from Hidden Child Foundation's Vice President.
- Vice President agreed to act as recruiter for study.
- PI met with recruiter to introduce study and provide recruitment materials (see Appendix).

Screening of Participants

- PI provided recruiter with inclusion/exclusion criteria and screening questionnaire (see Appendix).
- Recruiter screened potential participants with study's questionnaire and referred eligible interviewees, providing telephone numbers to PI .

Interviewing of Participants

- PI telephoned eligible interviews to arrange a meeting (either at home of participant or the headquarters of the Hidden Child Foundation).
- PI introduced study and obtained consent (see Appendix).
- PI interviewed consenting participants for 60-180 minutes, digitally recording the interview of eight participants.

Member Checking

- PI transcribed interviews verbatim and mailed copy to participant, along with two additional copies of consent: one blank and one signed, and a stamped envelope addressed to PI.
- PI requested that participants communicate any changes or edits to transcript in writing, returning additonal signed consent form in the stamped envelope as confimation of receipt of and approval of transcript for use in study.

Use of Data

- PI assigned psedonyms to participant data and consents.
- All materials with identifying information was stored in locked file cabinet.
- PI selected six of eight interviews for inclusion based on theoretical saturation.
- PI analyzed six interviews using the Listening Guide.

Inclusion Criteria

Study criteria excluded individuals under the age of 65 or over the age of 90 and excluded suicidal participants or those institutionalized for medical or psychiatric illness at the time of the study. Age limits were determined by the requirement that participants were between the ages of 1 and 18 years during the Second World War, which was guided by current life expectancy demographics (retrieved from: //esa.un.org/unpp/). All participants must self-identify as Jewish, be between the ages of 65-90, and have been born in European countries that were later occupied or dominated by Nazis during World War II. In addition, they must define themselves as a Hidden Children of the Holocaust, having lived in Nazi-dominated Europe. They must have never been in a concentration camp. Finally, individuals must pass a screen-out instrument assessing dementia (a short form of the Alzheimer's Disease Assessment Scale's Cognitive Subscale). The study's referral source conducted the screening of participants with the aid of a researcher-provided questionnaire consisting of the exclusion/inclusion criteria outlined here (each of these instruments can be found in Appendix). This minimized the potential negative implications of asking screening questions on the vital relationship between the researcher and the participants.

Alzheimer's Disease Assessment Scale- Cognitive Subscale

The ADAS is a scored rating instrument designed for the evaluation of the degree of severity of cognitive and non-cognitive dysfunction in people with Alzheimer's, rating the range of dysfunction from mild to severe dementia. The cognitive subscale (ADAS-cog) consists of 17 items examining cognitive components of memory, language, and praxis. Each item is rated on a scale of severity of dysfunction ranging from 0 to 5 (0=no impairment, 1=very mild, 2=mild, 3=moderate, 4=moderately severe, 5=severe). Item numbers 1 (a global rating of the quality of spontaneous speech), 2 (a rating of the ability to understand receptive speech), 4 (a rating of the individual's difficulty in finding desired word in spontaneous speech), 5 (rating of the individual's ability to carry out one- to five-step commands), and 9 (rating of ability to orient accurately to the date, month, year, day of the week, season, time of day, place, and person) were pulled from the ADAS-cog as a screen out for dementia for this study. These items were chosen due to their ease and speed of administration and scoring. Items 1, 2, 4, and 5 were used to determine a solid base of receptive and spontaneous language ability relevant to orally sharing a narrative and responding to the interviewer's probes. Item number 9 determined the individual's reality-testing and ensured the participant is orienting appropriately to the study's interview setting. A score of 2 or more errors (see reasoning below) rendered an individual unfit for the current study, and was the basis for the exclusion criteria. (No participants were ruled out on the basis of this measure). Examples of cognitive domains rated in this shortened form of the questionnaire include *Spoken Language Ability*, *Comprehension of spoken language*, *Word-finding difficulty in spontaneous speech*, *Following commands,* and *Orientation* (Rosen, Mohs, & Davis, 1984). The measure's normative data has been established for older adult controls, guiding this study's rule-out criteria of 2 or more errors (Graham, Cully, Snow, Massman, & Doody, 2004).

Reliability and validity for this measure has been well-established, and the measure's sensitivity to severity of dementia has rendered it a popular and widely used tool in the assessment and treatment of demented elderly (Weyer, Erzigkeit, Kanowski, Ihl, & Hadler, 1997). Interrater reliability for this measure ranges from .65 to 1.0, and Spearman test-retest correlations ranged from .58 to .92. The internal consistency of the ADAS-cog scale score is .81. The scale exhibits convergent validity with related measures such as the Dementia Rating Scale and the Memory Information Test (Rosen, Mohs, & Davis, 1984).

Data Analysis: The Listening Guide

The interviews conducted for this study were analyzed according to the Listening Guide, a qualitative data analytic method developed by Gilligan, Brown, and their colleagues (Brown & Gilligan, 1992). The Listening Guide is a rigorous, voice-centered relational method that entails a minimum of four consecutive "listenings" of the narrative. This method allows for the investigator to attend to multi-layered, complex communication and uncover psychological logic and intrapsychic process. It is designed to extract themes and examine both the directly stated content as well as the underlying, unspoken content. This method has been applied in a variety of psychological studies (e.g., Mauthner, 2000; Raider-Roth, 2005; Way, 1998; Way, 2001). Each sequential listening allows the researcher to understand different aspects of the participant's story, which when told in a relational context, reflect a cultural and societal framework resulting in richer understanding of the survivor's narrative (Gilligan, Spencer, Weinberg, & Bertsch, 2003).

The preface to the first step in this method involves examining one's question and uncovering the question's roots in one's individual experiences. Because the Listening Guide assumes a dynamic psychology, one must attend to the whole relational dynamic, which involves the researcher's stance regarding the question being posed. As this method assumes, it is impossible for the researcher to have no effect on the interviewee's response, as they exist in relation to each other and are interacting in the process of data collection. Therefore, in exploring and revealing the personal roots of one's question, one brings the bias to the forefront, engaging one's subjectivity (C. Gilligan, personal communication, March 28, 2006; Way, 1998).

Once the narrative has been transcribed verbatim, the official first step, or first listening, in the analysis is *Listening for the Plot*. In this step, the interviewer analyzes, line by line, the narrative of the interviewee, accounting for the overall landscape of the story. The goal of the researcher here is both to document the stories being told and to document the plot of psychological terrain, documenting the answers to the questions, "How does the interviewer know where she is psychologically?" and, "What are the distinguishing features of the psychological landscape?" (C. Gilligan, personal communication, March 7, 2006). In this step, the researcher must also attend to where one maps oneself in relation to the plot of the narrative. Qualitative researchers have asserted that it is critical to "attend to our own responses to the narrative, explicitly bringing our own subjectivities into the process of interpretation" (Gilligan, Spencer, Weinberg, & Bertsch, 2003, p.160). This step reflects the notion that the interview is a particular moment between the interviewer and interviewee that could never occur again in that way.

The second step, *Listening for the "I,"* entails listening for the voice of the self. In this step, every "I" statement is pulled from the narrative and documented as it occurs in a temporal sequence. These statements entail only the "I" and the verb following the "I." These statements are lined up on a page, creating an "I poem" that tends to fall into a cadence thought to illuminate the individual's inner psyche. These I-poems "pick up on an associative stream of consciousness carried by a first-person voice" (Gilligan, Spencer, Weinberg & Bertsch, 2003).

The third step of the Listening Guide method, *Listening for Contrapuntal Voices*, requires the researcher to examine the narrative and attend to the different voices in the interviews that are speaking to the research question. This step is based on the notion that individuals often have complex ways of speaking about their experiences that do not fall easily into a dichotomized, discrete category. This step allows the researcher to account for the multiple voices in which people speak. The term "contrapuntal" comes from the musical notion of counterpoint, when two voices move in and out of each other in relationship (C. Gilligan, personal communication, March 21, 2006).

The final step of the method, *Composing the Analysis*, involves assembling the evidence from the preceding listenings. In this step, the researcher is harvesting evidence from data that speak to the question, discovering the complex information provided directly by the interviewee and through the uncovering of the narrative in the previous steps of the method. As the researcher connects the evidence and the questions, the questions evolve and change, reflecting the newly discovered knowledge (C. Gilligan, personal communication, February 19, 2006). This notion is consistent with "garbage can" model of qualitative analysis, which "recognizes the importance of interconnection and interaction among the different design components" of the research (Maxwell, 1996, p.3).

As each narrative was analyzed and the listenings were compiled, the analysis of that individual narrative was compared with the preceding analysis/analyses to look for common themes that cut across informants. Each interview's analysis inevitably influenced the researcher's approach to the successive interviews in terms of relational dynamics, flow, and probing questions. The proposed semi-structured interview probes found in the Appendix served as a guide to communicate the intent of the study rather than a rigid protocol. As previously stated, saturation was employed (Way, 1998).

Again, this method is based on the necessary elements of subjectivity—the narrative exists in a relational framework between the interviewer and the interviewee. For this reason, interrater reliability is neither present nor relevant. As the participant and interviewee co-research, they are creating meaning that would not be expected to be replicated in a different environment with two other people in a different relationship (Sandelowski, 1995). The Listening Guide method requires that the researcher account for her own bias and role in the meaning-making in the analysis, accounting for the relational dynamics just as a chemist would account for her laboratory's temperature and humidity. In this way, this method's validity relies in making public that which factors into or confounds any psychological study rather than pretending that the researcher's presence and relationship to the subject has no effect (C. Gilligan, personal communication, March 7, 2006).

Criteria for Evaluation

The notions of reliability and validity, while always crucial when evaluating research, do not apply in the traditional sense for this qualitative study. The relational framework of interpretation is based on the belief that knowledge is subjective and co-created in social interaction and therefore is not expected to be stable and consistent over time, nor replicable in different circumstances or in different relationships with other researchers. Therefore, trustworthiness replaces reliability and validity. According to this notion of trustworthiness, research is simply argument, so evidence is evaluated on the merit of that argument according to the criteria of credibility, transferability, dependability, and confirmability (Lincoln & Guba, 1985). The trustworthiness of the findings of this study was evaluated based upon these criteria.

Credibility is established, in part, through the investigator's ability to learn the culture of the participants (without becoming overly immersed in it) in order to determine the relevant aspects influencing the data. Engagement with the participants' culture, when coupled with the investigator's use of tools such as triangulation, member checking, negative case analysis (looking for and at disconfirming evidence with regards to emergent theory), and peer debriefing (the use of a peer who takes an uninvested, outsider perspective look at the evidence and challenges the investigator) all contribute to the study's credibility.

Transferability replaces the notion of external validity. As Lincoln and Guba (1985) explain, "the naturalist… can provide only the thick description necessary to enable someone interested in making a transfer to reach a conclusion about whether transfer can be contemplated as a possibility" (p.316). In other words, the investigator must present the evidence that permits the reader to understand the context of the findings, and whether or not these findings may apply to other persons in other contexts.

Dependability, according to Lincoln and Guba (1985) may be reached a variety of ways, but for this study was determined through the use of an auditing process originally conceived by Halpern in 1983 (as cited in Lincoln & Guba, 1985). According to this process, the investigator created an audit trail of documents, audiotapes, transcripts, and working notes of every step in the investigation. Upon completion of the study, the selected auditor (in this case, a fellow student of the Listening Guide technique was used) examined the audit trail to determine various aspects including that appropriate linkages have been made, that methodological shifts in the emerging framework are supported, and that conclusions are parsimonious and supported by data, among other criteria.

This auditing process, along with the investigator's own process notes in a reflective journal, were combined to also satisfy the fourth criteria, confirmability. In line with the Listening Guide technique, "the reflexive journal might be thought of as providing the same kind of data about the *human* instrument that is often provided about the paper-and-pencil or brass instruments used in conventional studies" (Lincoln & Guba, 1985, p.327). The investigator repeated the auditing process until the auditor's complaints were addressed to the satisfaction of both the investigator and the auditor.

Ethical Issues

While this study does not directly question the participant about her Holocaust experiences, such subject matter is related to the probes and arose in some cases. The possibility of risk in this study was low, and none of the participants indicated that they experienced increased psychological distress upon the sharing of memories of Holocaust events during the semi-structured interview. While the investigator was prepared with a list of counseling resources and support groups (found in the Appendix), none of the participants requested services.

CHAPTER IV

RESULTS

What follows are Listening Guide Analyses of six interviews with hidden children. The analyses are constructed from three distinct listenings, or components: 1) Listening for the Plot (who is this person, what is her relationship to the Holocaust, what is the landscape of her narrative); 2) Listening to the I-Poems (following the psyche by listening to the participant's use of "I" chronologically throughout the narrative); and 3) Listening for Contrapuntal Voices (the distinct voices that arise in the participant's narrative). The Listening Guide calls for the researcher to examine the roots of her question, and in so doing, reveal her own bias. The epistemological assumptions underlying this project posit that all knowledge is co-created. As I subjectively explore each survivor's narratives, I must reveal how I have come to the question at hand.

Roots of My Question

I entered the office of my first participant, Sonia[·], as an eager doctoral student in the early part of my training. "I have read on this topic," I thought. "I know about trauma." I had my question typed in black, bold print on a clean white sheet, *Is it better to express or repress your trauma, and why?*, and recapitulated, *When is it healthier to repress, and when is it healthier to express?*, along with a list of other related questions, in the event that I became stuck or

[·] Some names and details have been changed and obscured throughout to protect the privacy of participants.

needed to redirect the conversation back to my question. Despite this, I had somehow managed to hold on to the naive and largely phony belief that I was taking a position of open listener standing on a plane of not knowing or believing which is better, and that she, as the expert, will enlighten me. I have repeated this mantra to myself for the entire journey to her office: "she's the expert." I never pulled the sheet from my bag, because it was already tucked neatly in my brain, sandwiched between the mental files I had been compiling for many months: one of which I called "expression," and one I had termed "avoidance."

My mental file on "expression" was filled with literature on trauma, on the Holocaust, on the century-old wisdom of the therapeutic benefits of integration, "talking it out," Freud's Case of Elizabeth von R (recently re-read), and the no-longer-so-new societal push to "speak out!" Following the wisdom of Freud when he first delved into the uncovering of trauma with Elizabeth von R (and in uncovering, healing her), I myself wondered that given Sonia's trauma, would she be dissociated, lacking identity, as traumatized people often are, unable to provide insight into my question? Would I need to dig and search through the material that she provides in order to find what it is I am looking for?

As Freud pondered in *Studies on Hysteria*, "When one starts upon a cathartic treatment of this kind, the first question one asks oneself is whether the patient herself is aware of the origin and precipitating cause of her illness. If so, no special technique is required to enable her to reproduce the story of her illness" (Freud, 1895). While not ill, Sonia had endured trauma, and I wondered about her ability to accurately recount and identify the roles of expression and avoidance in her path to recovery. Would the Listening Guide be my "special technique"?

The second, opposing mental file, "avoidance," was filled with literature on dissociation (which I had drawn on the other end of a continuum, opposite integration), data-supported studies indicating the detrimental effects of talk therapy, and popular media articles reflecting or suggesting the "new shift" to "Repress Yourself" (Slater, L., NYT 2/23/03). The score, and I had been keeping score, was not tied; avoidance had recently taken the lead. For me, the scales began to tip upon my reading of George Bonanno's American Psychologist article in January of 2004, in which he boldly identified a new path to resilience: avoidance. For some, the ability to compartmentalize, inhibit emotions, and move on from trauma seemed to lead to better outcomes and fewer PTSD symptoms. This spoke to me; I am an avoider.

I had found solace in the happy medium I had created in my mind. I had found my own way of theorizing the gap between the two camps of "expressors" and "avoiders": perhaps in a protective and adaptive move, the psyche unconsciously avoids and inhibits only until talking, expression, and integration become safe and viable. Maybe we are naturally enacting that which is the least threatening to our mental health, and for each person, that threshold is different. I was hoping the hidden children I would interview would lend insight into the debate and help me reconcile the two sides.

Without fail, each woman's first question was: *Are you Jewish?* The tone was always the same, as if coming from a place of confusion- seeking to make sense of some paradoxical pieces of information. My family name at the time of the interviews was "Jacobs," a traditionally Jewish name. Yet here sat an Anglican-looking young woman with straight blonde hair. I was nervous to field this question; I am not Jewish.

I was certain that I would be regarded with suspicion and anticipated my participants' reactions: What will you use this for? Can I trust you? Will you understand where I am coming from? Why are you interested in the Holocaust? I therefore responded to the first question not with a single response ("no"), but with an elaborated explanation of my longstanding interest in Holocaust studies that began in middle school, when I was simultaneously horrified in learning more about the atrocities and riveted by representations of the Holocaust in the media. I was struck then, and still am, by one thought: *but how could this have happened?*

I have since come to understand my reaction as akin to what Judith Herman refers to as the dialectic of trauma: "the conflict between the will to deny horrible events and the will to proclaim them aloud" (Herman, 1992, p.1). My disbelief was a way of denying the horrific capacity of the human spirit to destroy; yet at the same time, I was compelled to read more, to hear more.

I will never know how the questions I asked, the voices I heard, or the meaning I've made would have been different had I been Jewish, had I deflected the question, or had I not attempted to communicate my desire with a transparency bordering on apology. Nevertheless, my response to the question seemed to be, at the very least, sufficient for my participants to begin to speak about their experiences. I began to listen.

This astonishing and instructive experiment served as my model. I decided to start from the assumption that my patients knew everything that was of any pathogenic significance and that it was only a question of obliging them to communicate it… 'You will see something in front of you or something will come into your head. Catch hold of it. It will be what we are looking for.' -Sigmund Freud

Sonia

On the other hand, should a young person feel that the environment tries to deprive him too radically of all the forms of expression which permit him to develop and integrate the next step, he may resist with the wild strength encountered in animals who are suddenly forced to defend their lives. For indeed, in the social jungle of human existence there is no feeling of being alive without a sense of identity. – Erik Erikson

Sonia invited me via email into her psychotherapy private practice office on a weekday mid-afternoon. Her warm message, "a friend of [your advisor] is a friend of mine," confirmed the time and location of the interview. I trudged through the snowy slush to her office in Manhattan. As I walked past the doorman and down her building's stairs to her office, I felt nervous as this was to be my first interview, and my participant was a psychoanalyst. Is my question relevant? Will I be a good listener? Will she be able to talk? Will I be able to hear and handle what she says?

I knocked on the door and heard a voice inside, inviting me in. As I entered the waiting area, Sonia emerged from her office, smiling as she welcomed me and shook my hand. Sonia is an older woman with graying hair, but her round, baby-face defied her age. She spoke with a quiet, yet steady voice and still had traces of an accent. She was dressed stylishly, all the elements of her appearance matched and coordinated, down to her earrings. She sat down comfortably in a chair, inviting me to sit next to her on the sofa. As I placed the tape recorder on the table in the corner between the chair and sofa, I noted that this must be how she sits with a patient. I wondered about the dynamics of our seating positions in light of her psychotherapy practice.

As we sat in her office, I noticed how quiet it was- we were the only two there. I felt a certain sense of loneliness in this quiet basement room, as it was devoid of the noise and distraction that is common in life in New York City. I felt a sense of calm radiating from Sonia, and the room in which we sat seemed to suit her perfectly.

As we began our interview, I heard her moved by my question, challenged by it, interested in it. Her words came in a flood as she responded to my brief statements or questions with long and rich passages. She seemed eager to speak and had much to say.

Who Is She?

Sonia began her narrative by explaining the voice her parents gave to their own Holocaust traumas; her father as an escapee from a concentration camp, and her mother passing as a Catholic widow, hiding her husband in the attic of their apartment. She immediately revealed the "survivor status" of her parents, indicating that discussion between them and other adults was sanctioned:

> My parents talked about the Holocaust with, uh, between them, they are both survivors but also with, um, friends, many of their friends were survivors or people who had come to the United States before the war but they were from the same community.

She returned to the voice of her parents throughout her narrative, who not only expressed to each other and to their friends, but also to the world. Sonia mentioned several times how her father told his story: "in fact my father had written a memoir." She returned to and repeated the production of her father's book like a refrain, as if underlining his ability to express: "And during the hiding years, he wrote his memoir. His memoir was basically the experiences that he had been through in the concentration camp- that was the focus of the entire book." And again, "you know as I said, my father's writing and publishing the book, basically what he did was publish the book in 1975," sending it to the printer to be mass produced and released out into the world, expressing the trauma he endured.

Similarly, her Mother's voice was expressed to the public:

> In fact, my mother said, my mother was interviewed at one point in the mid 80's for [sic] video Holocaust archives and I remember from her script, you know what she, um, they did a videotape and I had a chance to see that videotape and uh she said that, uh, she and her friends would start to talk about anything ... and it seemed no matter what they were talking about, somehow they would end up there, talking about their trauma.

The value and degree of importance both of Sonia's parents placed on their own expression of trauma was obvious, as they were drawn to talk about it.

Sonia juxtaposed her parents' need for processing their own trauma and ability to speak and identify as survivors against the silence imposed on her, which stands in stark contrast. Her parents talked to each other, to friends, through memoirs and testimonies, and yet, "I as a very young child I was given the injunction against speaking." This injunction came from the very parents who she has just characterized as outspoken and expressive: "my parents sort of acted as if I was so young I couldn't possibly remember or deal with these things so they, um, they really discouraged any kind of expression about it or even, uh identification as, uh a, a survivor."

Her language, “my parents sort of acted as if” indicated that Sonia may have had a certain level of confidence in her ability to “remember” and “deal,” but her parents wrongly assumed, even pretended (“acted”) as if this was not the case, and she responded by rejecting her own survivor status: “I didn't see myself as a survivor for many years.” However, Sonia revealed that her rejection of status was not due to her own lack of knowledge or identification: “it’s not like I had forgotten or, um, didn't know about my history, I think it was always accessible to me.” Perhaps her parents' "act" was their own protective denial of the harsh reality that their daughter had been traumatized.

Sonia asserted that talk of the Holocaust “was forbidden at my house,” explaining, “there was such a strong injunction in my family against speaking about it, or even just acknowledging it.” However, given the voice her parents gave to their trauma, it became clear that the order for silence was only imposed on *her*, and talk of the Holocaust "was forbidden" only if it involved Sonia. An “injunction,” which means literally “a formal command or admonition” and comes from the Latin “to join,” is most commonly found in law language, which “prohibits the defendant from taking a particular action and maintains the positions of the parties until there is a hearing to determine the matter in dispute.” (retrieved from http://dictionary.reference.com/search?q=injunction).

An injunction is usually time-bound (“until”), but for Sonia, there never was a “hearing,” quite literally. Her parents never heard her case: her memories of the trauma, her identity as a child survivor, or her feelings regarding the experiences of the Holocaust. Nor did her parents speak to Sonia about their trauma: “Every time, uh, I would ask my mother questions, she would start to cry, so you know, that effectively ended any, any questions on my part.” They didn't "join" her in her silence, nor did they invite her to speak. The message sent was: don't ask, I won't talk to you. Similarly, although her father had written a memoir to be published, "I didn't know anything about his story. I mean, I think I sort of breathed the air and I knew he had been in a concentration camp, but I had no idea what he had endured." This lack of communication on the part of her father was not limited to the trauma, either: "and my father was very closed and very distant, and we didn't talk much anyway." Sonia was treated as if she'd had no part in the Holocaust, despite her role, "we were hiding my father, um, in the, um, in the early forties and I was told to keep the secret of his existence." If one cannot admit the trauma, if the injunction is never lifted, one cannot take action to repair the damage.

Splitting

Sonia's resulting confusion and struggle with her own identity in the face of the injunction her parents imposed became evident in following her voice, a guide through her psyche. Her I-poems revealed Sonia's struggle between being and not being:

I am not
I am not
I think
I
I was
I am
I was told
I don't know

I mean

I was
I was
I was
I was
I was

She explained, "and yet, I wouldn't have identified myself as having undergone trauma, so there is something ironic about that." The irony lies in the knowing and feeling drawn towards identification with trauma which she endured and remembered, ("I was drawn to, even in my friendships, I was drawn to people who had suffered"), but the rejection of that knowledge ("I was told/ I don't know"). This confusion of identity created a split, a split that Sonia identified as dissociation:

If I was
I couldn't
I didn't

I had
I think
I didn't

If I did
I mean
I think
I was dissociated

For her, the opposite of integration is a split between feeling and thinking. While Sonia remembered, and knew of her trauma, she was not integrated. For her, integration lies in the ability to give voice to that which she knows and infuse it with feeling. She explained, "I mean I think I was dissociated, but for me, dissociation wasn't, uh, forgetting. It wasn't like the repression that you mentioned. It was more a kind of disconnectedness from the feeling." Her doubts and confusion arising from the silencing of her voice resulted in an emotional distancing from the knowledge of the trauma. There is evidence of her intellectualization and psychic numbing as she described her time of silence with words of thinking without feeling:

I think
I think
I think
I think
I would

I think
I think
I think
I am not so sure

Contrapuntal Voices

This split became clear and sharp when listening for the Silenced Voice and the Expressed Voice in Sonia's narrative. By tracing these two voices, it became clear that almost every word she uttered came from one of them. Her narrative paralleled the journey she described from a time of confusion, doubt, and lack of identity (Silenced Voice) to a time of knowing, self-assuredness, and feeling (Expressed Voice), as each voice dominates its own place in her story, standing in contrast to the other.

In the Silenced Voice, when speaking about the period in her life through which she remained silent and disconnected from her trauma, Sonia's story was qualitatively different than that from her Expressed Voice. Her language: "injunction," "hidden," "disconnectedness," "closed," "discouragement," "damaging," "backfire," "err," "forbidden," "blocked," "deadness," "floated through," "without feeling real," "breathed the air", "afraid to go more deeply," and "deep hole" is language of imprisonment, the Holocaust itself. This Silenced

Voice reflects the *murder of her voice*, the traumatizing effects of which are becoming more evident. Perhaps this murder of voice was as traumatizing to her as enduring the Holocaust.

The Silenced Voice reflected the injunction against speaking and all that came with that denial of identity and trauma. A passive, disconnected, and dull (almost dead) tone arose in the passages in which she described her silence. Here was evidence of an absence of emotion that accompanied the silence. It seems that expression of voice is therapeutic and integrative only when emotion is involved, as she explained: "I am painting, although I painted before too, it has a different feeling now. It's almost like, I think what I experienced for so many years which I didn't know I was experiencing, was a deadness. And, and I feel like I have been coming alive."

In silence, or even in emotionless voice, she was dead. The inanimate nature that characterizes the Silenced Voice was revealed in her language: "I had the images… the memories came in the form of like snapshots or images." *Still life*. She explained: "it was as if I floated through the experience… without ever really feeling, without feeling real," noting her distance from the events and from herself. She is alive only when her voice is expressed, and with feeling: "it was as if I floated through the experience of high school without ever really feeling, without feeling real. It's a hard thing to describe, because I was, I did fine, I had friends, I enjoyed my art classes, but it didn't feel like I was real. That is probably the, the consequence of, of unexpressed trauma."

In her time of silence and "unexpressed trauma," Sonia sounded much like

Holocaust survivors who had suffered to the point that they experienced a death of the soul, and while appearing to be functional and living, they had disconnected from feelings and relationships to the point of becoming the "walking dead." Sonia's pain was palpable as she cried at the expressed realization of her unreality and "deadness." This death was evident only in her time of imposed silence, which revealed a direct link to the denial of the voice of feeling, knowing, and experiencing trauma.

The Expressed Voice, which arose like a phoenix from the ashes of her silence, in contrast, reflected action, movement, birth, growth, and life as Sonia described her time of speaking in her own words ("accessible," "connected," "permission," "momentum," "explore," "healing," "come to terms," "emotions flow," "cumulative," "painting," "growing," "I could write," "coming alive," "depth," "I will not stop this process"). This is the *Living Voice.* The Expressed Voice reflected the desire to speak, and the expression of self and trauma. This is the vibrant, living side, which was infused with feeling. A shift from the thinking and numbness to the language of emotion and movement was again obvious in listening to Sonia's I-poems:

I feel
I have become

I had no idea
I could write
I am painting
I painted

I think
I experienced
I didn't know
I was experiencing

I feel
I am coming alive

If dissociation is, as Sonia defines it, thinking without feeling, evidence of integration may be found in the expression of thoughts and emotions together in connection with the self. As Sonia described finding her voice in speaking of her trauma, the split began to be undone:

I was
I was
I felt

I just feel
I think
I felt
I did

And:

I felt
I could
I think
I think
I think

She poignantly described the reunion of emotion with thought:

> As you can see the emotions flow now. They were so blocked for so many years. That is one of the most interesting things that I have found, that, but you know I could talk about these experiences but, like a robot. And now, it has sort of swung, the pendulum has swung to the other side, and its very, very emotional for me; sometimes just a word or a thought will trigger a lot of tears.

The Struggle to Speak

This "pendulum swing" to emotion, expression, and integration seemed to come after a long and hard battle against the Silenced (and Silencing) Voice, and there was evidence of this struggle both within and paralleled by Sonia's narrative.

Her Expressed Voice, while initially absent or barely heard in the beginning of the interview gradually grew louder over time, emerging from under the dominance of the Silenced Voice. Just as this process was gradual in Sonia's life, "it began very slowly but has gathered momentum… so that now, I feel totally immersed in the entire experience but it began very slowly," so was it gradual in her interview.

In the beginning, the Silenced Voice reigned for the majority of her story, and her Expressed Voice, while emerging occasionally, quickly retreated: "I think that before that there was such a strong injunction in my family against speaking about it, or even just acknowledging it [SILENCED] and every time, uh I would ask my mother questions [EXPRESSED] she would start to cry, so you know, that effectively ended any, any questions on my part [SILENCED]." Even while the injunction was an understood rule, Sonia initially attempted to struggle against it, but was silenced once again, defeated. These two voices were at war with one another. The Expressed Voice again seemed to be defeated: "I didn't talk about it. [SILENCED] And if I did talk about it, [EXPRESSED], it was without any feeling [SILENCED]." Sonia's attempts to give voice to her trauma were repeatedly shut down by her parents, even up until their deaths: "I mean I wish today I could you know, ask some questions and talk to him and of course he is gone, as is my mother."

Sonia's struggle to speak was also evident in the frequent disruptions in narrative content: the almost rhythmic "um's" and "uh's", the stutters, the pauses as she searched for words:

> But, uh, even after the war, there *was, um, my,... my* parents sort of acted as if I was so young I couldn't possibly remember or deal

with these things so they, *um,* they really discouraged any kind of expression about it or even, *uh,* identification as, *uh, a, a* survivor.

Sonia explained in the beginning of the interview, "I am not always comfortable speaking," and she identified the source: "in fact my difficulty speaking I think is totally related to your question as well because I as a very young child I was given the injunction against speaking." These dysfluencies in her speech are evidence of the impact of silencing her voice continued to have on her. She seemed to lack confidence and comfortability in her ability to express herself at times: "yeah, yeah, that's what I was trying to say," as she laughed nervously.

As she moved deeper into her narrative and talked more about integration and voicing herself, however, the dysfluency became less frequent. This may be indicative of her difficulty speaking, which was greater before she became more integrated and began voicing her trauma. While the dysfluencies appeared to become fewer, they were still evident in both the Silenced Voice and the Expressed Voice, indicating that her difficulty speaking, as she noted, was still with her, even in expression of trauma and voice.

As Sonia told of her growing ability to express as she became more integrated, the Silenced Voice began to wane along with the dysfluencies, and became juxtaposed between longer passages from the Expressed Voice: "he [my husband] just naturally started to ask them [my parents] questions about the Holocaust [VOICED], he didn't know he wasn't supposed to. He didn't know that that, that it was forbidden at my house [SILENCED]. So anyway, I think that had a lot to do with [the ability to explore my history], feeling safe [VOICED]." This indicated her move deeper into integration, as the longer Expressed Voice passages frame her Silenced Voice.

Aiding Expression

Over time, Sonia's gradual struggle to give voice to her trauma was aided along the way from various sources, some of which she identifies in her narrative. The first factor she names as enabling her to speak is society:

> First of all there was more of an awareness of Holocaust issues. I think that, you know you mentioned the silence after the Holocaust. I think about, thirty years, really ... its a long time, after the Holocaust, then films started to come out, books.... That's one of the things. And of course the other was the fact that there was a growing, very slowly, but a, a gradual interest in, in the Holocaust. I think the society has a big impact on whether, um people are um, encouraged or discouraged from talking. I think there was a feeling in the early years after the war that nobody really wanted to know. That it was… first of all that they wouldn't understand if they heard about it. And then, if they, if they, even if they attempted to understand, there was, um, people's responses were often so unempathic [HMM]. And I think that there was a discouragement, of um, people were afraid.

As she explored this reason, there was a repetition of the word "Holocaust"- stunning compared to the virtual absence of it elsewhere, yet here it appeared four times in just as many sentences. Her use of the word "people," rather than "I," ("...people are, um, encouraged or discouraged from talking;" and "...people were afraid") when giving reasons for her lack of expression of trauma implied her disconnection with these reasons. Her lack of ownership, interestingly, followed this repetition of the word "Holocaust." Perhaps this move to distance herself from the word represented her ongoing struggle in identifying as a survivor. Sonia had difficulty communicating her survivor status earlier in her narrative, begging the question: "So now would you consider yourself a survivor?" After tiptoeing around the declaration *I am a Holocaust Survivor,* she seemed to believe she had already stated it as she replied, "Yes, that's... I certainly would." Her ability to connect and identify with the Holocaust seemed still compromised, despite her progress in expression.

Sonia went on to connect in the first-person voice again with that which aided expression as she named her relationships with her husband ("So, anyway, I think that had a lot to do with it, feeling safe"), her child ("Um, when my daughter was born..., and um also seeing her and remembering me at those ages that she was going through I think connected me with that experience also."), and her patients as helping her tell her story of her traumatic past: "But I think that interest first of all in going into this field, and then the interest of working with people who had suffered you know, and had gone through some tragedies, I think was um, my way of sort of moving towards healing myself and beginning to face and come to terms."

She returned to this first person voice as she mentioned her connection with others in an authentic and trusting bond that led her to speak. Given the support from people she identified (child, husband, patients), it seemed that none moved to silence her. Her husband, who endured trauma as well, ("even my current husband is a trauma survivor in his own way") spoke openly about it, even with her parents. Presumably with her child, she could start fresh and establish her identity as she defined it. In the absence of such an injunction in her close connection with others, she found she was free to speak. Indeed, relationships with others were tied with expression:

I had
I think
I first really began to talk
I
I connected

I remember
I had a chance
I have found
I could talk

In this Expressed Voice, enabled by connection with others, came integration and repaired sense of self.

Trauma and Healing

In contrasting the two voices in their distinct melody, it is clear that Sonia identified nothing adaptive at all about her silence and repression. There is only a lifeless, emotionless recounting of her "life" when her voice was silenced. She did not choose to stay quiet, she was ordered to. It was not an adaptive process she consciously employed to cope with and recover from her trauma.

The question of why talking has become "adaptive" in the face of trauma over time seems unrelated. In Sonia's answer to the question, the frame is shifted. This project's question is grounded in the notion that both avoidance and expression were likely necessary and adaptive; yet in listening to Sonia, it becomes clear that silence and avoidance was never adaptive, only harmful. The literature in favor of avoidance suggests that the ability to move on without facing trauma may be healthy, adaptive, and productive. This is exactly what Sonia did for a long time, but this is what caused her the most pain, ultimately traumatizing her further. On the surface, for a long while, it looked as though this was best for her. She was "fine, she had friends," but as Sonia explained, it was no kind of life.

Eventually, the trauma took its toll on her, and was compounded by the denial of it, as the denial of the voice became the denial of Sonia's identity. In this interview, Sonia gives voice to her most painful trauma: the long period in which her voice was murdered.

Instead of discovering the adaptive and necessary role of both avoidance and expression for Sonia, I have discovered the trauma of denying one's voice. Is this experience unique to Sonia? Do victims need to give voice to their trauma to become (and not to simply appear) truly healthy? Perhaps this is the trauma of children, like Sonia, were hidden during the Holocaust. As her narrative closes, there is evidence of a woman fully integrated, feeling, and solid:

I feel
I feel
I mean
I am

And yet, the journey is not over:

> When you talk about integration, it does, it feels more like, it is my history. I, I like to think that I will not stop this process, I won't get to a point where I say, okay I will stop this process. I won't get to a point where I say okay I've dealt with this.

Sonia reflected that one doesn't ever fully move on; one doesn't talk about trauma, and then it's over. One doesn't express in order to get over it. Sonia talked to continue living and growing, and to stay connected to who she is. Healing for Sonia came not from moving from her past, but in changing her relationship *with* the past, and this change and healing came with her ability to give voice, emotion-filled and personal, to her trauma. Sonia's expressed voice connects her to others, allowing them to learn from her.

Anita

Then when the others had gone, each man about his business, Robin turned once more to the youth. 'Now lad,' said he, 'tell us thy troubles, and speak freely. A flow of words doth ever ease the heart of sorrows; it is like opening the waste weir when the mill dam is overfull. Come, sit thou here beside me and speak at thine ease.' –Howard Pyle, *The Merry Adventures of Robin Hood*

Anita impressed me as a vibrant, colorful woman whose zest for life was reflected in her creative and interesting clothing and jewelry. Anita agreed to sit with me at the Hidden Child Foundation headquarters at the Anti-Defamation League (ADL), and her decision to meet with me seemed a simple and logical one for her- she did not equivocate or deliberate before offering an interview. Much of what she shared in her interview had to do with her life's current activities, rather than distinctly focusing on the past. She is a self-possessed woman who communicated a strong sense of her personality: "I was always very lively. Very lively, very talky, you know, and always everything's very positive. I don't have a negative personality."

Who is she?

Anita explained that she had hidden with her mother and sister in Poland in a barn for two and a half years, after which she immigrated to Canada and spent time in a displaced persons camp. Aside from these basic facts, Anita did not discuss her experience during the Holocaust, as she was accustomed to avoiding the details ("I would say I was hiding for two and a half years in a barn and that was the extent…nobody ever knew"). Anita explained that she did not speak to anyone about her experience until many years after the war, and after a window of time speaking about it, she has decided that speaking is not for her ("I am certainly not exactly—not the talker, you know"). This assertion stands in contrast to her initial claim of being "very talky," revealing the contrast in her talkative nature and her tendency to avoid talking about the Holocaust. In her role with the Hidden Child Foundation, however, she is integrally involved in empowering other hidden children to tell their stories.

As an adult, after many years of silence, Anita joined a group run by an early leader in child survivor trauma treatment. She attended her first meeting and decided she "was not ready;" she didn't return and "when you're a part of a group, if you leave the group, there's a betrayal." Anita eventually "felt ready" and went back and participated in the group, which gradually transformed into the initial core members of the Hidden Child Foundation. Anita brought the group to a national stage when she gave an interview about her experience as a hidden child for a major publication. Soon she began to field calls from around the world. Individuals from across the globe discovered that others had experienced the Holocaust as hidden children, and they were eager to share their stories. Anita listened to them with an almost religious conviction ("I became so focused on the Holocaust and I became so obsessive about it"). She estimates that she listened to at least 3000 people callers in response to her story ("I was very involved in it. I answered practically—I was so obsessive about it that I wanted to speak with everyone"). Despite her desire to "speak with everyone," Anita received the calls and served as a listener more than a speaker.

Her former life as an artist was put on hold as she dove in to work with the Hidden Child Foundation. While she has decided that she does not wish to talk much about her Holocaust experiences with others ("I never talk about it," "I want to keep it separate"), she ultimately believes in the healing power of sharing one's experience. This belief continues to drive her in her position at the Foundation, and is central in this interview.

Safety in Numbers

When reflecting on the experience of child survivors, Anita noted the prominent role of shame, and in particular, how this shame contributed to the silence so common for child survivors. Anita explained that the shame comes from a sense that one is abnormal or doesn't fit in:

> I heard over and over again the children who are abused also feel ashamed of it. They take the shame upon themselves. Victimization and shame—somewhere they're connected. Being different. You're keeping something that nobody can understand. It's a secret. It's more of a secret than shameful. Maybe that's not the correct word [shameful] but it's a secret. I don't want anybody to know because they'll look at me and I'll be a different outsider. I'll become an outsider.

Anita revisited the notion of shame throughout her interview ("They take the guilt upon themselves or they're ashamed;" "When you're younger, you're embarrassed. You're ashamed, you know?" "We've come from a different world and we were ashamed of what happened to us"). Again, Anita noted the shame was coupled with a feeling of not belonging, "com[ing] from a different world;" "an outsider." As a child, to be an outsider is often the last place one wants to be, so it is not surprising that one would want to hide differences, especially traumas, from the world. Differences threatened the safety of fitting in.

This sentiment was not relegated only to childhood for Anita, however. As an adult, she experienced intense feelings of shame when she "came out" as a hidden child to the world in a major magazine. She explained:

> [The magazine] interviewed seven [hidden children]. And speaking about that, we didn't want to be interviewed. We didn't want to reveal ourselves. People didn't want to reveal their jobs. They didn't want anybody to know—it was so distorted that we are so different. That we are – these victims. You don't want to be victims. You want to be normal. You know—you always want to belong to the group. You don't want to be separated by someone-something like, 'Oh my God, you're a Holocaust survivor.'—or, you know, it's like, 'Oh my God, you have AIDS?' or 'you are very ill? You have cancer?' You just want to blend into the life—into the world, I think.

Anita again expressed her desire to fit in, to "blend," to "belong" and not be "separate." For Anita, being separate was akin to a terminal illness or a death sentence. Here Anita shifts from the first-person "I" prominent in earlier passages to the collective "we." This shift reiterates her desire to be part of a collective; to have allies in her struggle. Her drive to be normal and to be perceived as normal motivated her to remain silent about her experiences during the war.

Survivor Status

While Anita noted that she did not want to be labeled and ostracized because of her experiences, she also paid attention to the damage resulting from being denied status as a survivor. This ban on speaking out was different: not one chosen by Anita that could be lifted at her discretion, but rather an imposed silence by other survivors. She described an ethos she observed and was victim to: if you were a child during the war, than you did not suffer as others had suffered and thus have nothing to say on the matter. She articulated this: "Nobody asks-nobody asked—especially with the young ones it was even worse because the notion was when you're young you don't remember." The assumption was that children couldn't relate to the plight of the survivor, so the possibility of their suffering was not addressed: "We were just so different that there was no support to make it legitimate, so to speak." Anita's experiences were deemed illegitimate, which likely magnified her shame and sent the implicit message: 'you don't fit in.'

This imposed silence was intensified by a second layer of assertions from the survivor community and society at large: "a Holocaust survivor was a concentration camp survivor," not "a child that had to hide his Jewish identity." Anita explained:

> There was a hierarchy in terms of Holocaust survivors. And the concentration camp survivors supposedly at the time were considered the only survivors… and my husband said I was not a Holocaust survivor. We were not given the opportunity to express ourselves in the context of a survivor community.

Again, Anita moves from "I" to the collective "we," seeking affiliation with the group in the face of being invalidated as a survivor.

Anita was told she was not what she felt herself to be, and understood that no one would recognize her as a survivor, nor would they invite her to speak about her experiences. This unspoken message further encouraged her silence, and influenced how she identified herself:

> We had to compartmentalize certain ideas. I think this is normal under the circumstances. I looked at Holocaust survivors as different. I didn't see myself as a victimized person. I would say 'them.' I was different. You see, I was much on top of it. I was beyond it.

Here Anita moves from the collective "we" to the isolated "I," this time distinguishing herself from the group. She makes an effort to differentiate herself in relation to other victims, again in an attempt to be "normal," average, and healthy; different and better than the victim. Anita internalized the sense that the trauma she experienced was invalid, and in fact, she derived strength from this notion. Again there is evidence of Anita's drive to fit in and be normal, which is meant to set herself apart from survivors.

Later in life, however, Anita joined a group of survivors and found solace in a shared voice of hidden children. She explained:

> It gave me dignity [listening to other hidden children]. You see, we didn't feel dignified before. We felt victimized. We felt less. So when I saw these people—wow. You know? These are Holocaust survivors. I fit in here.... I looked at these people, and I was so gratified that they are normal human beings.

Anita found her identity as a hidden child in the voice of others like her who were speaking out. Now she can again become part of a collective with other survivors (as evidenced in her intertwining of "me," "we," and "I") because the collective has "dignity" and is "normal." Her ability to find a place, and a group of people, with whom she could belong *and* retain her normalcy gave her a sense of pride about having endured her Holocaust experience that she had not previously had. By fluidly coming into and out of relationship with other survivors, she felt protected from feeling too freakish or damaged.

Anita's desire to be part of a group played a large part in her identity, and in both her silence and speaking as a survivor. Her focus on the collective is striking throughout her interview. The pronoun “we” appeared more in Anita’s interview than in any other interview conducted for this project. It is clear that Anita derives strength from being part of a community; fitting in with others contributed to her resilience. Anita explained that when the war began, she was older than other child survivors she knows, and that meant she developmentally was ahead; she “had already become part of a community. A lot of these children had never been a part of anything.” Being “a part” of something was a key protective factor in the face of trauma: “Even though I was young I was part of the community and I knew where I belonged. I was part of a culture.”

The importance of being part of something larger is reflected in Anita’s I-poem, revealing its impact on her identity and resilience:

I said
I was
I was
I
I
I knew
I belonged

I was
I was
I have
I was able

Here is evidence that the belonging lends itself to a sense of who Anita “was” as an individual (“I”).

Contrapuntal Voices

Realizing she was part of a group enabled Anita to break her silence and begin to give voice to her experience, but the act of speaking was incredibly painful, as is reflected below. In the following figure are some of Anita's words on the role of speaking in her life since the war.

Anita's voice of "Speaking"

SPEAKING
• I had to get up and … as soon as I said my town.. and my name, I became hysterical. I became very upset. I cried. • When we had our meetings… everybody worked out their problems… so there was a lot of fighting. There was a lot of carrying on. A lot of screaming…. We were abusing each other. We were insulting each other at meetings. • I would speak—I'd cry because it was so overwhelming. But I'd keep on coming back. • So I went [to a meeting]… and that's where I became very upset. • My father was killed in our house. .. every time this came up—that was the most traumatic thing. I was hysterical. I cried… [another woman in the group] thought I was so out of it that I needed to be institutionalized. After the thing was finished, I was myself again. It was just too- too much for me. • I went in [to a therapy session]—I thought I was going straight into—into the Holocaust… when I was finished with the session, I went in the car and not only did I make notes but I wrote pages and pages—I have probably five notebooks like this. And then I would read and I'll be crying and crying. • Well, there's a full page on me when I was 12 years old, in the magazine, a full page. I was- I was hysterical when I saw it. It was very upsetting. I mean, you're opening yourself up to the world, and then my story plus other six stories. So I had—I thought that some of my colleagues, uh, friends will call me. Nobody called me. Do you know what I thought, they didn't want to talk to me anymore. When I think about it, it like sounds ridiculous. I was overwhelmed. • But certainly coming back to [the past] was a very, very painful and difficult thing. • I found that [speaking] without the notes was too painful because I would really have to go right back there—I would experience it. I would have to retrieve my experience… I go there, but when I read it, I don't go there. But after awhile, every time I would do that, I would be sick for three days, so I don't go and speak anymore. I'd be so upset. • [at an exhibit on the Holocaust] I wanted to show the little segment from Spielberg that I'm on. I got so upset my heart palpitated maybe for an hour. I was very—oh, upset. For one hour my heart was beating and I was upset. • I am certainly not exactly—not the talker, you know…. I responded that I was upset. That was the only time ever anyone knew. • So some [speak in order to not be forgotten or insignificant]. I don't have [that] reward because when I speak… I get upset, and I don't want to get upset or upset people. I tried to minimize it for me.

Speaking

In her "speaking" voice, Anita reflects the sheer agony that accompanied the act of sharing her hidden child experiences. It is as if speaking her past aloud brought on all of the emotions one would expect from a child in the midst of trauma. There is profound sadness (repeated descriptions of "crying"), overpowering affect ("I was overwhelmed;" "too painful;" "it was too much for me"). There is also an element of interpersonal acting out in Anita's description of verbal disclosures ("fighting;' "carrying on;" "screaming;" "abusing each other;" "insulting").

One begins to understand Anita's experience of speaking as a violent spilling out of uncontrolled, and uncontrollable, affect. The out-of-control nature of the telling of experience is captured in her language, as she repeatedly uses the world "hysterical," and even noted that others got the impression that she "needed to be institutionalized" when listening to her express her trauma. There is a sense that the speaking functioned not to control or contain the emotion or make sense of one's experience, but rather to indiscriminately expel affect like a surging spigot. It is as if speaking has the power to annihilate, just as it did when Anita was a hidden child.

As Anita reflected on "speaking," she most frequently used the word "upset" to describe the emotional pain experienced during her telling of her past ("upset;" "very upset;" "very painful and difficult;" "very upsetting;" "I would be sick for three days;" "so upset;" "so upset;" "I was upset"). Her use of the word upset draws the listeners' attention to the notion of balance. Indeed, in speaking,

Anita's balance was upset. While Anita asserted that she believed in the therapeutic power of talking and telling one's story, her own experience of speaking was wrought with agonizing, uncontrollable affect that threw her off-balance. In the voice of speaking, Anita primarily uses the pronoun "I," which, when compared to the rest of her narrative, stands out in contrast. This suggests that speaking is an isolated, isolative experience for her; one that offers no solace in being a part of a larger group. Speaking is an assertion of identity absent of a protective "we."

On the other hand, Anita reflected on the role of "silence" in her life:

Anita's voice of "Silence"

SILENCE
• They [adopted hidden children] were not forced to, but they were advised to – advised to forget the past and not talk about it • Children who were simply not given the opportunity and their experience was minimized and they never spoke about it • It was so traumatic and there was no psychological intervention at the time- there wasn't such a thing. It shuts itself… It shuts itself off. • I guess in order to accommodate those emotions … I had to shut it off • I hadn't—I – I never talked about it • Nobody ever knew my past • We were just so different that … there was no… support to make it legitimate, so to speak. And in fact, I think the world was silent. Jewish people who found it different to talk about the losses… everybody shut it off. • We never talked about each other's experiences. It was something that we just blanked out. • We didn't know each other's stories. We didn't. We were just moving forward. • We were in such shock, we were so traumatized, it was overwhelming… the brain shut down. Shut down completely. To cope with the present, the life that we were so fortunate to be given. So part of shutting down was not talking about your experiences. • That was a past that was shut and done. • I heard stories like husband and wife [who] were both survivors and never told each other. It was—just too difficult to open up that aspect in any intervention. • I said [to myself] 'that's strange, why can't you see?' It was a washout. I mean it was just too overwhelming. No one thought—there was no

intervention here. Nobody asks- nobody asked—especially with the young ones it was even worse because the notion was when you're young you don't remember.

- We invited [a hidden child] over to be the keynote speaker. He didn't want his family to come. It was just too painful to—to strip yourself open with those emotions, I think.. it's just too overwhelming. You show all your vulnerabilities. You show yourself in a very painful way, and I guess we don't like to do that.
- You think about your mommy and you think about your daddy. And they say, 'don't talk about them because I have a new life.'

Silence

Silence, on the other hand, has a distinct sound of protection against the turmoil, upset, and violence evident in speaking. The protective nature of this repressive silence is reflected in her strikingly frequent use of the pronoun "we" in comparison to her "speaking" voice. This voice is absent of her own lived experience; she uses "you," connoting a more generalizable sentiment. In silence, Anita doesn't have to own the trauma. In her use of pronouns, Anita reflects that she does not feel alone in her silence; she is joined by others, which makes her feel protected. In fact, being silent allows her to be part of "we."

Anita's voice of silence was of "forget[ting];" "blank[ing] out;" "washout;" "minimiz[ing];" and most prominent- "shutting off." Again and again, Anita returns to this notion of "shutting:" "It shuts itself… It shuts itself off;" "I had to shut it off;" "everybody shut it off;" "the brain shut down. Shut down completely;" "shutting down;" "That was a past that was shut and done." This notion of "shutting" is referred to in the active voice, as if one's volition played a part ("I had to shut it off;" "everybody shut it off"), as well as the passive, involuntary voice ("it shuts itself off; the brain shut down"). Regardless of the role of volition, the use of the word "shut" suggests that trauma can be enclosed like a room, and the door shut to divide it from the rest of the psyche; the surging spigot is turned off, and no longer has the power to annihilate.

This door and room metaphor continued as Anita explained that the trauma was "just too difficult to open up," and it was "too painful to—to strip yourself open with those emotions." This is a different type of silence; not silence encouraged by those around her nor silence chosen to by Anita in order to fit in. Instead, this silence was psychologically protective, enabling the trauma to be cordoned off and isolated in a separate room, as if quarantined, where it wouldn't leak out and poison the rest of the psyche. This silence sounds more like dissociation, where painful aspects are split off and isolated from interaction with Anita's consciousness. This split is evidenced by one of Anita's I-poems:

I guess
I had to shut it off
I hadn't
I
I never talked about it

I would say
I was hiding

Anita's use of the word "hiding" brings into focus that silence recapitulates the hidden child's experience during the war. Just as silence was protective and vital while Anita was hiding, hiding continues to be protective. Anita hides from the trauma by shutting it off in a separate room, splitting it off and silencing it.

Dissociation

As she reflected on her trauma, Anita remembered: "I used to dream a lot about it. I didn't talk about it but I used to have tremendous nightmares. I would run, I would hide. I found a method- I would fly… I found actually a good method. When I had to run away in my dream I used to fly actually. In my dream I would actually fly away." In her dreams, Anita would escape, flee, and hide. In her waking life, she seemed to be doing the same. She explained:

> I have two people… I was this little girl. And then there's this camouflage, that person's another person who adapts to the world, who becomes part and extension of this contemporary world, you know? And tries to become part of it. So, that child in me was there, but now it's, I don't know what to say. We act on two tracks. One track is my Holocaust experience and the other one is my real life with my family—with my life as I have developed it.

Anita's use of the word "camouflage" reiterates her need to blend in; to hide was analogous to "adaptation" for her. Anita referred to her life as "on two tracks." She split her trauma from the rest of her life—what she refers to as her "real" life. Her use of the word "real" suggests that Anita has quarantined her trauma and minimized it to a lesser status than her other life experiences. It is as if her trauma does not exist in her present-day, "contemporary world," but rather is part of her past, stopped in time, and stored elsewhere. Only by hiding, or camouflaging herself, can Anita live a real, adaptive life.

The split between Anita's "contemporary world" and her trauma was most striking when she reflected on her intense re-experiencing of both bidden and unbidden memories. When Anita is in the throes of speaking about her trauma, she seems to be unable to exist in her present-day psyche, in her "contemporary world." She described an instance of speaking about her trauma in a group:

> My father was killed in our house. .. every time this came up—that was the most traumatic thing. I was hysterical. I cried… [another woman in the group] thought I was so out of it that I needed to be

> institutionalized. After the thing was finished, I was myself again. It was just too- too much for me.

Anita declared that while she may have split off her trauma and cordoned it in its own space, she cannot be rid of it by "shutting it off:" "When things implant themselves into the brain, they're always there. They can be triggered and they cannot be removed." Anita referenced the uncontrollable nature of this split off trauma: "It was another person's choice. It's not like you intellectually say, 'now I'm going to think about my…' it just made—it just says, 'hello, I'm here.'" Anita's passive helplessness is evidenced in her language ("implant," "another person's choice"). She is being victimized by the part of herself that has been traumatized. Although Anita shut off her trauma, she was unable to silence it. She explained, "I think that one does not have a choice. I think when this kind of faced itself and came forward it was not an intellectual decision."

Anita found, however, that choosing not to speak helped her exert control over the traumatic memories. Talking freely, without a script, to others about her Holocaust experiences brought Anita directly into the heart of the split-off room and face-to-face with the part of herself that contained the overwhelming, painful affect. She articulated her journey into the dissociated trauma:

> I found that [speaking] without the notes was too painful because I would really have to go right back there—I would experience it. I would have to retrieve my experience… I go there. But after awhile, every time I would do that, I would be sick for three days, so I don't go and speak anymore. I'd be so upset.

Although Anita broke her silence in an effort to break down the barrier between the two parts of herself (the trauma and the "real life,") she continued to struggle with her desire to hide, especially in the context of belonging to a group.

She reflected, “I never talk about it. It’s like, I keep those two [my art life and my hidden child life] separate. I don’t know why…[my fellow artists] don’t have any idea… I never talk about it. I want to keep it separate.” Anita says she “do[es]n’t know why,” but in listening closely to her, it seems that she keeps it separate in order to not stand out, but to fit in.

Integration

Anita noted that she “went through all this healing and all this talking” in an effort to integrate her trauma into her psyche. As she has moved toward integration of the split-off part of herself, she has recognized some detrimental effects:

> All these paintings which I did… I was able to somehow, I was able to condense my childhood… I was able to actually experience the joy which I did as a child. But when I went through the healing, I lost it. That’s a strange thing. You know what I’m saying? I thought about it. I was able to actually retrieve the joy—you know, the good feeling—but I think, later on, when I went through all this healing and all this talking, I can’t get to that place anymore.

Anita has begun to open the door to the shut off part of herself, and it is as if this has contaminated the previously protected “real” part of Anita that used to be able to contain pure positive emotions like the utter joy of childhood before the war. Anita lamented that she used to “remember this wonderful, wonderful—I can’t do that anymore, so I don’t know if that—the pain overwhelms the other part.” Just as speaking overwhelmed her like a rushing spigot, opening up her shut-off trauma overwhelmed her joy and positive emotions. Speaking annihilates just as it had the power to do when Anita was in hiding as a child. It is as if the dual selves that Anita has created (the "real" self and the traumatized self) cannot exist together.

The Therapeutic Value of Speaking?

Even in the overwhelming, painful, violent, traumatic experience of speaking about her trauma (as previously detailed in Anita's "Speaking" voice), Anita noted that she "kept coming back" to meetings of child survivors. Why? She reflected:

> Because we went through the same experience. Even now when we get together—you know, we had another life. And we all have, uh, memories of these horrors. And we don't have to speak about it. We come from another place. It's like you meet a friend from your town… they know your childhood and they know your parents. And there's a different kind of interaction. Whether we come from Poland or from Belgium—we went through the whole horrible stuff together. So that's a bond.

Interestingly, joining with other hidden children at meetings meant that Anita did not have to tell her story or declare her trauma; it is understood even in silence. In a way, the group relieved her of the burden of having to speak. Anita explained her attendance: "this pain center was already open because I already went there to begin with, you know? I made this first step." Reflecting on her early meetings with the group, Anita insisted, "It was something that I needed to do and I didn't want anyone to stay in my way." She explained why she felt compelled to go:

> I'll tell you, there was just a lot of anger. But people were able to permit themselves to do it in our presence. Because we absorbed it and we didn't turn away from each other. Because we needed that kind of—in whatever way it was expressed—we needed to come back.

This response captured Anita's belief that it is necessary to open the part that has been dissociated, repressed, or "shut off" with others in order to "come back." Again, with her use of "we," there are echoes of Anita's belief in the healing power of the collective; benefiting from being part of something. Anita revealed her belief that in the process of expression, one can eventually access split off parts of oneself and begin to exert control over and integrate what had previously been an expelled contaminant. The act of expression, even though traumatic, enabled Anita to gain greater control over her trauma. She explained:

> I know it's not a choice that I made [to finally speak out about my trauma], it was just driving me. [Now] I'm in more control. Sure, sure. It's like with the writing of my story. When you take- put something out, and you take it back in, there is already a process of change that takes place. That's why when I wrote it and cried over it I take it out and I can look at it from the outside in, so I think that's probably where the healing comes in, and right now after so many years, I am much more able to handle it. I am not only emotionally entangled, but I can intellectually manipulate it.

Initially, Anita sounds as though she is at the mercy of her trauma, which "drove" her, apparently, without her volition, to speak. The speaking was not an act aimed at recovery from her trauma, but rather is reminiscent of the surging spigot. Her passivity in the process of speaking is evident:

> Once the gate… my inner psyche opened itself up… I think it was a collective thing. When you get of a certain age, 50 plus, your resistance breaks down and you no longer can control that part of yourself which was suppressed. The other thing is you start reflecting, completing your circle. And you start reflecting on – on your whole life and that surfaces.

Again, the notion of the collective appears as Anita moves from "I" to "you" and "your," backing away from the personal experience of expression and reflection. She has a more passive stance, explaining that the shut-down trauma is "opened" due to the weakening or wearying of the psyche's ability to keep affect lidded and "suppressed," at which point the trauma "surfaces." While she has previously declared that the expression of trauma lends control, her language here suggests that the "opening" of her psyche is out of her hands.

Despite her passive role in the telling of her story, once "the pain center" or "the gate" opened, Anita was able to exert control over her trauma. Anita's personal agency is evident in her consistent use of the pronoun "I." Her ability to cry, write, handle, manipulate, and look at [the trauma] from the outside in has brought her healing.

Anita espoused the benefits of expression, but her choice of pronouns reflects that this is not a personal preference or strategy that she employed. Anita again distances herself from the act of speaking by using the pronoun *you*: "Well, perhaps if you had an opportunity to speak about them, it may be much more healing than just keeping it in your brain all the time." Her pronoun shift when talking about the healing power of expression suggests this is not her personal conviction. Likewise, when Anita expressed her belief that speaking one's experience out loud to others is reparative and rewarding, she moved to separate herself from the collective:

> Some people just love, love being on the Speaker's Bureau [of the Hidden Child Foundation]. And I said to myself you know it's a bonus, because when they speak, people listen. They're out there. So that experience, by itself, eventually it's a pay off…I don't know, you know, I have my glory. I don't need that, you know? But I can imagine people go up there… the satisfaction of having people listen to it gives you the desire to do it over and over again. I mean, you know…we are all people now and we become very insignificant, and when you go up there, people listen…I don't want to take away from the fact that some people feel a huge commitment to tell the story of the Holocaust so it not be forgotten. But by doing it…there is a reward. There has to be a reward. I don't have a reward because when I speak, first of all, I

> don't need it. It's not in my nature. You know, I feel very fulfilled, secure, whatever it is.

On the surface, Anita espoused her conviction in the therapeutic value of speaking, which is echoed in one of her I-poems:

I've told
I've told

I get
I don't

I know
I made
I'm more
I more
I'm just
I

I wrote
I cried
I take
I can
I think

I am
I am
I can
I tell

Her expressions—telling, writing, crying—are followed by assertions of identity ("I am"), competency ("I can"), and reward ("I'm more;" "I get"). She explained, "I wanted to speak to everyone. It was a process of personal healing."

And yet, a closer listen to the passage above reveals, at least, that Anita is ambivalent. In fact, talking, for Anita, has little personal therapeutic value. Those who speak are belittled. She stated, "I don't need that," but "they" and "you" find it rewarding and fulfilling, by implication, because "they" and "you" are less secure than Anita. Her distance from hidden children as a group is noticeable as she strives to distinguish her needs from those who speak about their experiences. It is in this distance from the traumatized group that one again hears Anita's desire to be recognized as "normal," not affiliated with this traumatized group. This differentiation from the traumatized group is echoed in her I-poem:

I looked
I looked
I
I saw
I didn't

I would
I was
I was
I was beyond it

I was having
I was
I was

I was so overwhelmed
I was so overwhelmed
I didn't want to tell

Here one can hear the recognition and then denial of her relationship to trauma, asserting that she is "beyond it." She is overwhelmed by it and shuts it down, not wanting to tell. Despite her complicated relationship with speaking, Anita reflected on the benefit she believes her voice has brought to hidden children:

> I can speak about it now. [This is] a huge difference. I wasn't able to talk. Now that I can speak about it openly… perhaps it's important, my contribution and people like me- like I am who speak, we leave some legacy instead of hiding behind and becoming self-focused only. We're doing something which is valuable, hopefully, by speaking and having—you know, the hidden child has become a generic name.

Anita speaks about leaving a "legacy" by speaking, and she implies that to remain silent would be to stay in "hiding." Hiding was the very trauma hidden children experienced, and silence would perpetuate this trauma. However, Anita's striking use of the word "generic" (literally, *relating to or descriptive of an entire group or class*) as a descriptor of hidden children highlights her striving towards ordinary, regular, usual (retrieved from: http://www.merriam-webster.com/dictionary/). Anita has used the power of her and others' voices to ensure that hidden children are no longer relegated to lesser status on the hierarchy of Holocaust survivors; indeed hidden children are now recognized, through her work, as group that "relates to" and "is described by" the genre *Holocaust Survivor*. In her use of this word "generic," however, she has also revealed her unending desire to fit in, to be normal and no longer separate, which has driven her silence as well.

Trauma and Healing

Through her narrative, Anita has revealed that the most disturbing and feared aspect of being a hidden child is to be thought different, aberrant and atypical in a world where fitting in brings her comfort and safety. Anita has shared how closely her identity is linked to the collective, and sites this connection to a community as one of the factors that promoted her resilience in the Holocaust ("Even though I was young I was part of the community and I knew where I belonged. I was part of a culture"). For Anita, what would make her "a different outsider" brought shame, as would be expected, especially in the time of adolescence. This desire to "blend" and "belong" continued beyond adolescence, and throughout her narrative.

Anita's desire to be a part of a group pervades her life today and continues to be a motivating factor in remaining silent about her Holocaust experiences ("I never talk about it; I want to keep it separate"). While on the surface, Anita acknowledges that speaking is important in order to leave a "legacy," to be less "self-focused," and to bring "personal healing," speaking about her trauma threatens her link to the collective; the group of "normal" individuals with which she needs to be affiliated to affirm her identity. When Anita gives voice to her trauma as an individual, speaking in the first person "I," one hears annihilation and imbalance. Trauma had to be "shut off" in a room, isolated from her psyche in order to retreat to the safety of "we," as heard in her voice of "silence."

Anita's narrative becomes powerfully clear when one examines its parallel with her Holocaust trauma. Indeed, as a hidden child, to speak out meant mortal danger. To stand alone as "I," different from "we" meant death for a Jew. To be unexceptional, part of the mainstream, one of a group was the safe harbor that hidden children sought as they denied their Jewish identities lest they be annihilated. Just like Anita's trauma, Jews were "shut off" in an isolated space, split off with no interaction with others, relegated to a silent, hidden existence. There was safety in numbers. *Don't stand out.* Given this parallel, one begins to understand why, though Anita promotes speaking as a pathway toward recovery, silence pervades. Her ambivalence is clear.

Connie

Silence propagates itself, and the longer talk has been suspended, the more difficult it is to find anything to say.- Samuel Johnson

I had first heard Connie's name several years ago as I embarked on this project. A prominent figure in the social circuit of survivors in New York City, Connie is a head administrator for the Hidden Child Foundation. I was intimidated to contact her but I knew she might be instrumental in helping me get an insiders' perspective. Not only was she a hidden child herself, she was in a sense the gatekeeper to dozens of other hidden children. I sent an email with a reserved hopefulness. I figured she'd be too busy to address my request for interviews.

Connie wrote back less than a week later. She said she'd be happy to help me; I was elated. We drafted a letter of support for my dissertation on behalf of the Hidden Child Foundation, verifying their indication that they would help me find participants, and she signed it and sent it back to me. We had several phone conversations; she was courteous and professional and easy to work with.

Unfortunately, a year had passed before I began work on my project. I feared my slow progress had compromised my chance to work with the Hidden Child Foundation. I called the office prepared to re-introduce myself and make my pitch all over again. Once again I was amazed and relieved to find that Connie remembered me well and we picked up where we had left off. Of course she would help me, she said, and we made an appointment to meet in person.

I arrived that summer at the Anti-Defamation League in a big corporate office building in midtown, and Connie came down to collect me from the lobby.

She was kind and friendly, though not verbose. Her bobbed brown hair gave the appearance of a woman younger than her chronological age. When coupled with the lines on her face, she looked as if she had her share of life experiences, though they hadn't killed her spirit. Connie was well-dressed and I admired her upright posture which lent itself to a sense of confident directness and youth. She offered me coffee and a pastry to share. I fumbled through some paperwork I had brought; I was trying to strike a balance between following protocol as I had outlined for the project and respecting her position, authority, and humanity. At this point Connie was to help me find participants, not to be a participant herself. But I found myself curious about her and began to wonder if she'd agree to be interviewed.

Over the next week, Connie called me almost daily with a new name and telephone number of a hidden child willing to participate in my project. I was eager to include Connie as one of my interviewees, but she artfully deflected my requests. While she never outright said no, she explained that she didn't know if she could offer anything for the project or in response to my question. "How could this be?" I thought. She was clearly a woman who was integral in her organization- an organization largely devoted to speaking out in schools and communities about their experiences in the Holocaust.

After several weeks of visiting the office to interview participants and many phone exchanges to pass on names of potential interviewees, Connie consented to sit with me and talk about my research. Among all of my interviews, I felt most personally connected to this one. Perhaps because we had a chance to get to know each other a little bit before I interviewed her, perhaps because I felt as if I had won her over, but I am convinced that a large part was because she made me feel comfortable in her presence. There was a straightforward, cut-the-drama element about Connie. She isn't overly-friendly but she is engaged and kind. She seems truly interested in others. She is a therapist by profession.

Who Is She?

Connie was reluctant to share many details of her experience during the Holocaust, yet in providing the basics several themes can be detected that lend cohesion to her story. Connie was 11 years old and living in The Hague, Holland when the war began. At that time, her father had already passed away, and she was living with her mother and brother in an apartment. A Catholic priest who was part of the resistance helped her family hide in various apartments with different individuals and families.

Connie's gratitude for those who provided safe havens was evident, though a closer listen revealed some anger and resentment regarding those whose motives seemed to be other than pure kindness. She described one such host: "so we went… where there was a woman in a little apartment who had, according to her, had sinned terribly, and she didn't want to go to hell, and she wanted to go to heaven, and she thought if she saved Jews, she might go to heaven. It was as simple as that." The woman eventually couldn't tolerate her own anxiety over hiding Connie's family, and Connie believed the woman invented a story that made it imperative that they leave. If the woman had been motivated by true concern about Connie and her family, she might have continued to hide them in her home.

The ulterior motives of her hiders were pointed out by Connie, tempering her gratitude with a sense of distaste. She explained: "In Holland you didn't call it rescuers, you called it hiding parents. These were my hiding parents. And my hiding father loved the whole thing. He was in his glory to find food for the family, find ration cards for the family. We don't really know what he did in the resistance. I mean, he was in his glory. This was what he liked to do. And after the war it was kind of dull. [Wow, that's a strange type of excitement to have]. Defiance." Connie indirectly ensured that these "hiding parents" are not unjustly glorified as "rescuers" by pointing out their self-serving motives. She was aware that her victimization was an opportunity for the gratification of others, which makes for a complex situation for anyone, let alone a young girl.

Her knowledge of their selfish motivations, when coupled with her gratitude for saving their lives, left Connie ambivalent and somewhat confused:

> My mother …kept in contact with our hiding parents… see, my feeling is that we are eternally grateful to them for saving our lives and risking their own. So you don't really know what to do. You know, you go visit them. You bring some flowers and a present but it's never enough, you know? It's never, never enough. And then later on, when their children were growing up more and were thinking more on their own and were maybe married and so on, one or two would say, 'we really suffered too.' And they did. Imagine that you have three people in a very small house living with you who you're not related to and everybody's life is risked because of these people [who] are there because of the father's decision. So there was resentment. One or two. A lot of resentment, you know? [That felt] bad… it's like I was innocent but I couldn't do anything about it. I can't make up, you can never make up, you know? And to be indebted to people is not a good feeling. They were strangers. They were strangers. I mean and now

> you're life-long connected to them. Luckily they were good people, you know. But still [it is] not a good feeling. It's very difficult, I guess, to explain why you can't walk away from it.

While Connie can empathize with the hardships of those who hid her, this empathy is like a burden that she attempted to relieve herself of by reiterating her utter lack of control and validating her role as a victim. She is a victim to the Nazis and a victim to those who hid her, mercy to their selfish whims that are gratified by keeping her family. She is frustrated that she seems to continue to be at the mercy of her hiders. She felt as if she owed a debt that she will never be able to repay, nor one that she'd want to: "Would I do this? The same they did? I don't think so. No, I think… well, based on how I'm feeling, you know… it wouldn't be excitement for me like it was for him."

Connie skipped over the telling of her Holocaust experiences, and explained that when the war ended, she returned to the Hague, where she finished school. She joined a Zionist organization where she met her husband, who had also been hidden during the war. They started a family and had two children - a son and a daughter. Connie noted that this period of life was devoted to moving on rather than dwelling on the horrors of the Holocaust: "[We were] busy working… and building up a country… we were very busy you know." When asked if she spoke about her experiences with her husband or her children, Connie replied, "No. We didn't. Our children say, 'you talked about it all the time.' I don't think we really talked about it. Not in detail."

Silence & Invalidation

Silence seems to be the hallmark of Connie's Holocaust experience, both in her life and in this interview. This silence seems to have been initially imposed in Connie's childhood and has since become a part of her ethos. In tales of her childhood, imposed silence was mentioned like a refrain. Connie told of the mandate not to speak: "had to be silent;" "you know, actually [the house full of children of the family hiding us] were not really told you can't talk about it. But they didn't. Nobody talked about it outside of the house. Amazing, you know? Kids knew;" "and my grandfather always said, 'Shh, don't – don't be so loud.' You know. And there were always German soldiers coming by on the street."

After the war ended, the injunction against speaking about the war continued: "My mother said that was the Hitler time and it's over;" "I didn't know that story. We didn't talk about that;" "And we didn't – with all the others who were – had been in hiding, and there were quite a few, we didn't talk about it;" "[My children] know bits and pieces. We didn't …like we said, we never talked about it. We – we didn't."

Not only was Connie impressed with a sense that she should not be speaking about her experience, there was also a suggestion that her experiences weren't worth speaking about compared to adult survivors: "My father-in-law set that kind of up. You know, he said, 'Oh, your mother suffered.' And the kids didn't. That was the implication. And then, um, I guess I came uh, became more aware of it." As a young adult, Connie came to understand that she did not 'qualify' for status as a survivor, which contributed to her tendency to move on, not look back, and remain quiet about her suffering.

At that time, Connie did not recognize that these messages from family and society were preventing her from speaking about her experiences; she simply thought that there was nothing to speak of: "We didn't even realize that we never would have a normal – whatever normal is—life because always something would be hanging, you know, like… you know, three years in hiding, uh, you know, does something to your emotions, you know?" These effects she came to gradually recognize over time.

Although Connie was not speaking directly about her experiences with her children, she noted that there were noticeable effects that her past had on her parenting. Connie remembered being particularly struck by memories of her past when her daughter reached adolescence:

> It was like, I couldn't, really, you now, my adolescence and her adolescence were completely different. And it was difficult for her and difficult for me because I had no model. It's because at that time, I was in hiding and my head was full of lice. I mean, it's like a little – different.

Connie compared herself to her daughter, and remembered herself as overprotective of her son. The impact of her Holocaust experiences was expressed indirectly:

> I think it was a reaction to us being afraid something might happen. Something bad might happen. So [the children] – they're both affected by it. Well, I was a little hysterical when they were, um… One time I saw, we had an – across the street there was a young kid, and they played, um, had a rifle… uh, and they were playing in the backyard and that kid was holding a rifle, you know. And it was touching my son's back, like my son was standing there and… I – I reacted so strongly, said, 'you get out of this yard!' – I

> don't know what I said, 'and don't ever come back with this rifle into my – my property.' I mean, I was like hysterical. Um, these kind of reactions, you know, when it becomes very like… it was like, umm, a picture I might have seen somewhere, you know, where the German Nazis, you know, were holding a rifle.

As Connie began to discover that she indeed was carrying scars from her experiences during the war, she began therapy, where she talked about the ramifications of the Holocaust on her life. She began to explore her connection to the war, and she attended a panel where members discussed child survivors who had been in concentration camps. Connie stood up at this panel and asked about hidden children, who had not been mentioned as child survivors. She noted, "I must have been ready [for recognition of the suffering of this population]." Out of that came an invitation to join others forming a group that would become the Hidden Child Foundation, and Connie was asked to lead a workshop. It began to occur to her that there was a population of people of which she was a part, who "were not heard." Connie notes multiple times in the interview that hidden children had been denied a central part of their identity: an acknowledgment of the role of the Holocaust in their lives. While many, like Connie, had come to recognize the effects of the war in their lives, they were encouraged to minimize or deny these effects, which led to confusion and anger: "I think I had enough of being—not being recognized as having suffered."

Connie, like many other hidden children, had been told to forget the past, as it allegedly had no bearing on children. The pain of being denied one's own experience, particularly one with such far- reaching implications and noticeable effects on one's life, is echoed in Connie's I-poem:

I think
I know

I lost
I don't know

I thought
I knew

I knew
I forgot
I was devastated

The injunction against speaking was a message to forget what she knows, and in so doing, she was "devastated."

Soon after attending the panel, Connie approached her boss (she was working as a social worker at the time) with the idea of leading a support group for other survivors. Her disclosure to her boss was one of the earliest "coming out" experiences she'd had:

> And I must have been thinking about it… wouldn't it be good to do a group for people like me? Maybe I can find them. I went to my clinical supervisor and I said to him, 'This is what I want to do.' I was talking to him, because I never really told him, 'yeah, I am a Holocaust survivor…' And I was so moved I could b—barely could speak. And he said, 'you must do it. Go ahead, do it. It's wonderful.' So it was like I was talking really about something that I had been hiding where I was working. I had worked with somebody very closely. He didn't know my history.

Being invited to speak about her experience by her boss was clearly a touching and transformative experience for Connie. The experience seemed to be influenced by the long-imposed silencing of her voice ("I could b—barely could speak") as she literally came out of hiding. She began to explore the hidden child's damage not only of the Holocaust, but of having one's experience be denied. She explains, "I started the group here…I thought that people would be able to talk about their Holocaust experience. Because we were not really recognized as Holocaust survivors." Connie recognized how empowering it was to find her voice, and began to strive for a place where others could speak up too.

Connie's self-assurance and pride blossomed as she began to speak out about her past. Her I-poem reflects this:

I started
I started
I thought
I knew

I
I was
I became
I guess

I started to talk
I know

Much of Connie's pride arises from her work to enable others to share their experiences. In her interview, that she now finds it gratifying to enable others to speak, but does not wish to speak much herself: "My husband talks a whole lot more about the Holocaust than I do. I don't talk a whole lot about the Holocaust. Um, although I'm in the midst of it here I still don't talk about it because I'm busy with other stuff." Indeed, this interview mirrors such a dynamic; Connie has helped me find hidden children who will speak about their experiences, but is reluctant to do so herself. The purpose Connie finds in enabling others to find their voice is heard in her I-poem:

I said
I started
I could offer
I was
I could do

Connie reflected on the hidden child support group and its purpose:

> [The group is] really not necessarily talking about my experience… but talking about the need for Holocaust survivors to get together and talk and we work something out. I think it was more an – an – a process of growing professionally and, um personally, it gave me, um, something that I felt I – felt good about what I had accomplished. Um, I knew more or less what was needed for people who had been in hiding. What kind of workshops they needed… I was a good advocate to say, you know, this is what is needed.. I mean, I think it gave me, besides my profession… another—I have a hard time kind of expressing it – something that has been very gratifying to me.

Contrapuntal Voices

Connie has lived in two worlds with regards to her Holocaust experience; she has been amongst the silenced, and has emerged as a speaker. She has ample experience as a listener, particularly in her role leading groups, and also knows what it is like to be the teller, or the "listened to" (or not listened to, as the case may be). Therefore, Connie is in a prime position to shed light on the role of listening in the sharing of traumatic experiences. Connie spoke about her experience of being heard and of hearing, and her thoughts on each are placed side-by-side in the following figure.

Connie's voice of "Listened To" vs. "Listener"

LISTENED TO	LISTENER
• "[My children] don't want to hear it. " • "We were interviewed by the United States Holocaust Museum– we asked them to make copies for our children. So my daughter apparently looked at it, watched it, and she said, 'I thought it was much worse,' after she had watched it. [Interviewer: You mean, she thought you had been through worse than you actually had?] Right.	• "You know, it kind of trickled in. I didn't quite want to believe it." • "I didn't – we didn't really hear – you know, it was so terrible what you heard so you didn't want to believe it." • "[My mother] might say something but not elaborate on it. And you left it. So if somebody would say

Because the fantasy – whatever she had heard she couldn't put together because of too many holes there, you know…" • "Um, they kind of always move back, my children, when my husband talks about it… push their chairs back. They don't want to hear it. It's too disturbing to – for them."	something and not elaborate you wouldn't question or pry, you'd just leave it." • "We weren't ready to hear. We had something. It was like we had a mission to live a normal life."

Connie's pain in not being listened to is striking. The "not knowing" of Connie's experiences creates distance in her connection with her children as they "push their chairs back" and "fill in" information about their mothers' experiences. There is a sense of rejection as they "don't want" the story she offered them. The story of Connie's daughter's reaction to the videotaped testimonial indicates that Connie's true experience has been actively dismissed and minimized. Interestingly, when listening to Connie's own account of her difficulty listening to the stories of trauma, one hears virtually the same language. Despite having endured trauma herself, Connie has as much difficulty bearing witness to it as her children do. Avoidance seemed the easier option for all.

Some subtle differences in the language she chose suggest that Connie has not drawn a seamless parallel between her experience as a listener and her children's responses to hearing her own story. Connie repeatedly referred to her children's rejection of the accounts Connie is offering them (i.e. "they don't want to hear it"). Connie's own refusal to take the trauma in, however, was self-described in less rejecting and more understanding language couched in a collective act rather than an individual choice (i.e., "we weren't ready;" "we didn't want to pry"). Also, she asserted that she indeed listened and heard, but "couldn't believe." This subtle difference suggests that Connie ascribed intention to her children's inability to listen rather than seeing it as an iteration of her own understandable, defensive response to the trauma. This likely contributes to Connie's feeling of injunction against speaking and invalidation of her trauma.

Connie's voice of "Listened To" vs. "Listener"

LISTENED TO	LISTENER
• "Especially my daughter is more affected by it than my son. Although with him you would hear him, um, when his children were small and we would say, 'Oh, watch out! Watch out! Nothing should happen to the child.' He would say, 'I don't want my children to be afraid.'"	• "And I don't know if we protected our self and the others [by not talking]. We don't –I – I don't quite know. I'm making – I'm thinking about it now. Uh, but we probably protected ourselves and them."
• "And one of the reasons why I think the healing—I have never thought about it really—um, was so delayed because nobody was listening. And people –really the therapist didn't – couldn't deal with it."	• "We didn't have a whole lot of empathy—with all the others who were in hiding, we didn't talk about it."

Again, Connie's own experience as a listener mirrors her painful account of feeling unheard. Both columns reflect the sense of protection the silencing can lend, and the lack of empathy that seems to be characteristic of the listener, whether the listener is Connie herself of the "other" listening to her. This brings into stark focus the bitter reality that to listen to trauma is a difficult, if not impossible task. The message sent by the listener seems to be *be quiet.* And even for Connie, who could presumably empathize with this difficulty as she had experienced it herself, there is pain, sadness, and a sense of rejection at being silenced or left unheard.

Connie's voice of "Listened To" vs. "Listener"

LISTENED TO	LISTENER
• Connie: "Is it hard for you [to hear]?" Interviewer: "It's hard—it's hard to hear the stories, but I also feel a responsibility as a listener not to push my chair back. You know, to stay even though it's difficult to hear." Connie: "Oh, it's very difficult to hear."	• "Oh, much later I thought about that. Not then. Couldn't—couldn't think about it. You know, it was like kind of, you know, in Holland they say, 'they didn't come back.' They didn't come back. It was a very convenient word not to face the horrendous tragedy."

Connie repeatedly related the difficulty in hearing and being present in the face of trauma. In listening to her pain and frustration in being silenced and feeling unheard, the question becomes: is it therapeutic to be heard? Has Connie's own suffering taught her how to listen better to others, so that they won't experience the pain she has by being silenced? How has she been informed by her experience of having her stories rejected by listeners?

Empathic Listening

When asked if being listened to and heard, even by someone who has not had a similar experience, is enough to provide healing, Connie equivocated:

> Well, [some say], 'No matter what. There's always some healing going on when you talk about it.' Do I agree with that? I think– some people—have such a hard time with healing, [they] have multiple traumas, cumulative trauma. I don't know how they can heal. Maybe a little bit? So, one of the reasons why I think the healing was so delayed because nobody was listening. And people – really the therapist didn't – couldn't deal with it, so you need to kind of look at it. If you go through a very traumatic time, immediate treatment would be a whole lot better than 30 or 40 years later.

Connie lamented that "nobody was listening," including, as was heard, herself.

She explained that participants in her hidden children support group "say it is fabulous. It's really—because people understand." Does the shared, common experience of the hidden children provide the key element in effective, therapeutic listening? Indeed, the realization that group members had experiences in common, not just the "talking," drove the formation of Connie's successful support group. She explained, "I must have become aware, uh, about that people who'd been in hiding were not heard prior to that, you know. And I must have been thinking about it… I can do a group, wouldn't it be good to do a group for people like me?"

Connie stressed the importance of being an empathic listener as she repeatedly referred to the aspects that made her ideal for the role of group leader (i.e., "You know, because I am so attuned to this;" "And I mean I was so attuned;" "I would make her feel comfortable;" "I was very attuned to it, but the people around me were not."). Her sense of being "attuned" is a result of her own experience as a listener, of feeling silenced, and of having endured the Holocaust as a hidden child. Her ability to provide therapeutic listening was rooted in the shared experience: "I knew more or less what was needed for people who had been in hiding." Connie elaborated:

> But see, if you do a workshop you only listen to a piece of somebody's history. And you treat it differently than saying, 'and where did you go then?' you know? You just kind of say, so… you know, 'how did you feel about it?' you know, and there is somebody else who has the same experience. Somebody was listening to them. Nobody listened. We weren't heard. So people didn't—at the conference, people didn't stop talking. You know. They just didn't stop talking because-- there was somebody who understood if you say, 'yeah, I was in hiding,' 'Oh yeah, I was in hiding too.' So it's people not only hearing you but also understanding somewhat and having empathy for what you went through.

In the group, talking was sanctioned, and the sanction seemed to uncork the silence. The words began to flow.

Interestingly, Connie's responses throughout this interview were peppered with frequent "you know's:" "Um… so that really was, us for us, *you know*, we really – that's what we wanted. We didn't even realize that we never would have a normal – whatever normal is – life because always something would be hanging, *you know,* like... *you know*, three years in hiding, uh, *you know*, does some harm to your emotions, *you know*?" Connie's use of "you know's" seemed to be bids for understanding, as they elicited frequent affirmations ("mmhmm") from the listener. In this way, Connie is acting out her need for validation from the listener, as this is what makes the telling truly therapeutic for her.

A Time for Talking

Connie indicated that the time directly following the Holocaust was busy with rebuilding and having a family. When asked if she would have been ready to talk 40 years ago, when she had wished for someone to listen to her, she reconsidered: "I don't know. Maybe not." When asked whether, given a magic opportunity, she'd to back in time a create a group like the one she runs now, Connie reflected on the role of timing in the therapeutic power of being heard:

> You know, my friend and I organized groups of younger children than we were… and they all had been in hiding… at the time I didn't know how to do it, really. I mean, I could do with a group you know… play games or whatever. Uh, I don't know, I think maybe – right now it feels kind of scary that everything was so raw, you know? You have to have—somebody needed to be extremely well-trained and – to open it up – this hurt and then be able to close it up again, you know… I don't—maybe it was good that people first, um, tried to live a normal life so they had something to fall back on and then open up? Especially children, I

> think. If I think of 9/11, um, people had families maybe to—you know, to – to support them. Some of these child survivors were orphans. They had no one. I don't know, maybe it was better not to talk…I can think about maybe… if you don't have a support system to fall back on, can you… that is scary, right? Uh, I really – I almost would say… I—I—maybe it had to be like this.

Here, "you know," in such close proximity to "I don't know," suggested both Connie's uncertainty about the best therapeutic action, and also reflects a childlike concession to authority ("I don't know" but "you know"). Again, there are echoes of invalidation. Her shift from first person ("I could") to second person ("somebody needed") is suggestive of her uncertainty in relying on her own experience. This demonstrates Connie's stance that she is not sure she can add to the conversation, just as she was not sure she 'qualified' as a Holocaust survivor.

Connie asserted, "maybe it had to be like this." Like what? She continued:

> Yeah, like what? That's a good question. Well, I was kind of – I might want to modify this a little bit. I don't know what length of time but there should have been some foundation. A support system that maybe – maybe it was good that, you know, people got married and had children and maybe then talked because then, there's a purpose to one's life. You have to go on. Children are waiting for you, you know.

Connie became more assured about what one "has" to do in order to cope effectively with trauma. She reiterated the need to move on, build a family and a foundation and a purpose in life in the time immediately following the Holocaust. She explained that the trauma, like a wound, was "too raw" to "open up" too soon after the Holocaust. Indeed, Connie's I-poem communicated this same message of productivity following trauma- moving on and building- instead of reflection on the past:

I was taking care

I worked
I cooked
I
I mean
I worked

I don't know
I
I don't quite know

I'm making
I'm thinking
I married

I was
I said
I would think
I was
I couldn't
I had no
I was in hiding
I was in hiding

I mean
I mean
I
I do

I don't talk
I'm in the midst
I still don't talk
I'm busy

This I-poem highlights the link between productivity and avoidance. By not knowing, hiding, and not talking, Connie was able to "take care," "work," "mean," and "do." Connie seems to be communicating that one cannot be productive and face and express trauma openly at the same time.

The question of whether to talk, when to talk, to whom to talk, and how to listen are all central questions that Connie has attempted to answer, though she still hasn't answered it to her full satisfaction. After all of her reflection on the pain of being silenced, and the healing power of being empathically heard, Connie still pays respect to the notion that sharing one's experience may not be the solution: "Um, you—you cannot be too fragile. You have to have some strength. I think, you know, because for some it's so horrendous, I don't even know… You have to have some defenses, too. A little denial, a little avoidance, a little—a little of all of it. No… you need a lot. You need—we needed a lot. Needed a lot."

Trauma and Healing

Silence is the cardinal trait that characterizes this interview. Connie related the imposition against speaking, first as a necessity to survival while a child in hiding ("'Shh, don't be so loud.' There were always German soldiers coming by on the street"). Connie's silence was not only essential to her own survival, but for that of her hiding family ("everybody's life is risked"). The mandate against speaking continued even after Connie was out of hiding ("My mother said that was the Hitler time and it's over"). Connie soon learned that despite her traumatic experiences, she was not to have a voice as a victim of the Holocaust ("My father-in-law…said, 'Oh, your mother suffered.' And the kids didn't. That was the implication"). Even after Connie began to explore and talk about her experience as a hidden child, she again received the message *don't talk about that*; her children rejected her story ("they don't want to hear it"), effectively communicating, *don't share this with me. Be quiet. Go back into hiding.* The consistent imposed injunction against speaking, "does something to your emotions," Connie explained. Indeed, it has invalidated her experience, something with which she still struggles.

Invalidation was something Connie was all too familiar with, both from her own experience of being silenced, but also from her own inability to face the atrocities, which she reveals in her voice as a listener ("I didn't want to believe it"). These experiences make Connie duly prepared for the empathy and attunement to the hidden child's experience she has located in herself ("I'm attuned," "I knew what was needed"). Connie "knew" that hidden children needed a forum to own their traumatic experiences; to be able to speak about what they endured in a space that sanctioned their voices and validated their status as Holocaust survivors. Connie, like Sonia and Anita, suffered from the denial of her voice. This suffering allowed her to address this plight for other survivors, as she knew better than anyone the traumatic effects of the injunction against speaking.

Although Connie knew this was needed for hidden children, she paradoxically rarely talks about her own experience ("My husband talks a whole lot more about the Holocaust than I do. I don't talk a whole lot about the Holocaust. Although I'm in the midst of it here still don't talk about it because I'm busy with other stuff"). Connie's story is primarily one of liberating the voices of others from imposed silence and validating them, rather than speaking herself. After so many years where silence was vital for survival, then imposed on her by others, invalidating her experience, it is no wonder that Connie would have complex feelings about the value of speaking about her traumatic experiences for herself.

Fran

Now I can look at you, Mr. Loomis, and see you a man who done forgot his song. Forgot how to sing it. A fellow that forget that and he forget who he is... See, Mr. Loomis, when a man forgets his song he goes off in search of it... till he find out he's got it with him all the time. - August Wilson, "Joe Turner's Come and Gone."

I came to know Fran not through the Hidden Child Foundation, but through a mutual friend. After some back and forth phone calls, we arranged for my visit to her apartment. She gave me meticulous directions. When I arrived, she ushered me down her apartment's dark hallway to a dimly lit living room, where we sat a small round dining table to commence our interview. Fran's apartment gave me a gloomy feeling, and while Fran was cordial, I sensed a hint of bitter feelings lurking just below the surface. She spoke in a hushed voice and as if in parentheticals, and I had trouble understanding her. I found myself having difficulty connecting with her, which stood in contrast to the ease I had felt with other participants.

Fran expressed some angry feelings and resentment as she told her story, immediately becoming concerned afterward that these sentiments would appear in her transcripts or published as part of this project. She instructed me throughout our first meeting to de-identify parts of her story or leave parts out altogether. I assured her that it was her right to take out or change any part of her interview; that I would be sending her a transcript which she could edit as she saw fit. This seemed to reassure her and the interview continued. At the end of the meeting, Fran arranged a time for me to come back to her apartment to discuss any edits she wished to make.

Unbeknownst to me, my then-boyfriend had planned a trip to surprise me during the time of the arranged second date with Fran. I had to cancel my appointment with Fran at the last minute as I had been surprised by a proposal! Fran was quite angry with my last-minute cancellation and reluctantly congratulated me, though explained that this was not an excuse to change plans. We agreed that Fran would make her edits to the transcript on the electronic document and email it to me, which she did. Fran expressed her frustration that the digital recorder failed to pick up many of her words- a problem I attributed to her manner of speaking rather than the equipment, which had captured other participants with crystal clear accuracy. Interestingly, more than any other participant, Fran was adamant about de-identifying her interview and omitting parts of her story—in effect, hiding her identity from the reader.

Who Is She?

Fran's interview is characterized by a sense of identity diffusion (discontinuity of the self), frustration and anger as a result of what she endured as a hidden child. She has endured a lifelong struggle to define who she is, so an effort on my part to introduce her seems to fall short, and fails to capture this struggle, which is integral to her identity. Fran was born to Czech parents in Italy. Her father died of tuberculosis when she was two, and she believes her mother became depressed as a result of the loss of her husband. After Fran's father died, Fran and her mother moved to France. During the war, Fran's mother dropped Fran off with a stranger at a train station before she was deported and killed in a concentration camp. This was the beginning of Fran's identity struggles: "I remember that, um, you know, [my mother] probably left me with this man in the station and then I never saw her again, and I think that sort of promoted, if you wanted, this complete disconnection, you know." Fran lost her connection with who she was before the war.

Like many Jewish children in Europe, Fran was placed in a convent orphanage to hide during the Holocaust. She shared a poignant story about her entry into hiding:

> In the convent, they realized—I mean, they gave me a false name… But my mother had embroidered my name on all my—all my clothing. And um, of course at some point we had to leave because it was dangerous, you know. I went through five or six places. And uh, that one of the nuns saw my name. And of course it was very dangerous. She started to rip it off. And I started screaming, you know. And that was the end, you know. I felt like I was finished. After that she took away – you know, my identity. So I think all of these things, one after the other, is a—in a way, uh, I just couldn't handle them. I didn't have it in me to handle it. So – I forgot. You know, I simply forgot. I think I also forgot to feel which was, which was not very good.

The disconnection from her life and identity as she knew it characterized her experience in hiding. Fran was unable to hold onto a cohesive sense of self as the nun "took away [her] identity:" "that was the end… I was finished." Fran's description of being "stripped" begins a metaphor that continues throughout her narrative; she was stripped naked of her identity. This was too much for her to bear: "I couldn't handle it." In her naked state, Fran subsequently "forgot" who she had been up until that point. The forgetting was an effect of the trauma of the loss of her identity rather than a chosen mechanism to cope.

While in hiding, Fran moved around and lived with several families before she was adopted by an older couple when she was eight years old. This nomadic life not only further stripped her of her identity, but she was cloaked with new imposed identities as she repeatedly attempted to adjust to new surroundings: "I was converted;" "I was all these different edicts;" "I had this new life." These new cloaks served to shroud and obscure Fran's identity: "they gave me a false name;" "I had… this old subterranean life which I progressively forgot." Her former identity was buried, and she was left disoriented: "I was very confused;" "I didn't fit. I felt like a sore thumb;" "It's still the, you know, it was just bits and pieces, you know, because, uh, basically, I think there was part of me, I have to say, that was broken;" "I was always torn;" "So, I am conflicted in my identity… I don't want to be swallowed up, you know." There is violence in her language as she describes the obscuring of her identity. Certainly, the stripping and subsequent shrouding of her identity was the trauma most salient for Fran.

Fran explained that her adoptive mother was a Buddhist ("an upper class hippie") who had no children of her own. The lack of emotional connection with her adoptive mother was clear in her description: "I was there at the end of the war, and it was like—I was like a present for her, you know. And I wanted the mother. She wanted the child." Her use of the article "the" added an air of triviality or facetiousness, reflecting a sense of failed idealization; her apparently unrealized wish for a mother and a home. Her reference to being a "present" is reminiscent of the effect of being covered and concealed, wrapped up in a box by, and for, someone else. This suggests that being adopted became yet another cloak over her true identity. Fran offered little else in the way of information about her relationship with her adoptive parents, except to say that they became ill during Fran's adolescence and she was charged with taking care of them.

Anger

Fran's anger about her experience as a hidden child – and the ongoing repercussions of this experience- was palpable. This anger reared its head throughout the interview as she reflected on her experience, particularly with regards to religion: "I sort of knew I was Jewish and always thought there was something wrong with that in a sense it was an enragement;" "I was furious to be Protestant;" "I had a problem with nuns because at the time they… made me feel really like a piece of garbage. … and then I was told the Jews killed [Jesus]… which really and totally enraged me. [I had] such a bad feeling about them. I mean, that was another reason I didn't want to talk about it. Because I hated them…. I hated them." Fran was enraged by the way in which her Jewish identity was forced to be concealed by new religions that eclipsed and denounced Judaism, one of the only remnants of her former life.

Even when Fran turned to religion as a safe haven and 'home' of sorts, she could not find safety, solace, or identity there either:

> I was very religious at one point and I was very much, um, involved with God and had written all sorts of thank you to God for saving my mother. Of course He didn't—so I obviously must have felt very betrayed. So … I became more like a—I'm sorry to say, like an automaton.

Fran's attempt to own part of her identity (her religious convictions) failed when she was betrayed; her mother was killed. When Fran describes that she then "became an automaton," it is as if she is saying that she gave over to the cloaks and disguises imposed by those around her, becoming literally *a machine that follows automatically a predetermined sequence of operations or responds to encoded instructions* (retrieved from: http://www.merriam-webster.com/dictionary/). Fran was filled with rage, but eventually gave over to the imposed identities. Her trauma is found in her surrender to the cloaks that obscured her identity.

Although she surrendered, Fran's anger continued to boil under the surface, ultimately prompting her to speak about her experience. She described becoming activated by her anger when listening to a forum about survivors: "They really talked about Holocaust survivors as a bunch of basket cases. At least that's the way it came across, and I was furious… it sort of gave me a jolt. And I thought to myself, I have to deal with this and that's when I decided to start my study on hidden children." This incident that sparked Fran to speak mirrors her own identity struggle. Survivors were being spoken about with sweeping statements that obscured their individuality and humanity, and like a "present," wrapped up in a "basketcase," closed and covered over.

Anger as a motivator to jettison the cloaks that had obscured her identity and speak out was also evident in one of Fran's I-poems:

I'm answering
I mean
I had

I progressively forgot

I
I sort of knew

I was Jewish

I was
I was furious

I grew
I really started to feel

I came
I
I could speak

In this I-poem there are traces of an identity struggle; ownership of an identity ("I mean/I had"), the effects of concealing that identity ("I progressively forgot"), the gradual reunion with identity that unlocked anger at how it had been obscured ("I was Jewish/I was/I was furious"), to the growing, reconnection with affect, and finally, an ability to speak out.

Contrapuntal Voices

Fran gave voice to the role of speaking in her life during and after the war, and also reflected on the silence that was more characteristic of her experience as a hidden child. In the figures below are Fran's reflections on both speaking and silence as related to her trauma.

Fran's voice of "Silence"

SILENCE
• I didn't know what I was so I never talked about it. • I had this new life and this old subterranean life which I progressively forgot. • It's like I lived on two different planes, you know. • Because that's the way I grew up. I mean I was a hidden child you know. I think you stay hidden. I mean, it's a comfortable place to be, you know. • And the Germans had come—I was in school and the teacher asked who is Jewish in the class. And I was with my little friend who was Jewish and she raised her hand. And for some bizarre reason I decided not to…I wasn't sure I was Jewish… But I did not raise my hand. And two days later my little friend was deported with her family. • But I was just—so confused and I-- I never talked about it. • I realized that I carry something around that I'll never be able to, uh, to address really. • Because there is a lot of shame in not being able to, you know, to tell—to

have a story and to tell a story. And so that's what also makes it imperative to speak. To try to have a story but to tell it in a way that other people can hear it. It's a connection to other people. It has to be a connection to other people. And if it's not then it becomes, again, something that's, uh, you know, poisonous. And I'm not exaggerating

- I worked in this school and I never told anybody anything. I had nothing to say, you know. And so when you don't speak—I mean, just as a hidden child, I feel I continue to be in hiding.
- When I was an adolescent, I think I had sort of almost a nervous breakdown because I didn't – not really, nobody knew, you know. I mean, I never talked about it. I mean, nobody understood.
- Suddenly it occurred to me, nobody ever invited me to speak [about my experience in France]. If I talk about it with my friends in France they way 'oh, enough' or 'forget about it.' They don't want to deal with it.

Silence

In Fran's description of her silence, there are echoes of the diffusion of her identity, disconnection, lack of integration, and forgetting. This reveals the integral role of silence in her most salient trauma: her identity conflict. This silence is not necessarily an injunction against speaking, but rather, Fran's sense that she didn't know enough about who she was to speak it: "I didn't know what I was;" "I lived on two different planes;" "I wasn't sure I was Jewish;" "I was just—so confused;" "I carry something around that I'll never be able to, uh, to address really." Her uncertainty characterizes her silence; the covering over of her identity as she went into hiding has obscured her self to the point that she no longer can give voice to her identity. Fran characterizes speaking as an "imperative connection to others," as if it would be reaching out from under the shroud to grab hold of another person who can help pull her out from under the cloaks over her identity.

Fran reflected that the act of hiding and covering over her identity as a child prevented her ability to form a sense of cohesion in her life: "you stay hidden;" "I continue to be in hiding;" "I progressively forgot." She is lost under the imposed layers. Indeed, Fran explained: "there is a lot of shame in not being able—to have a story and to tell a story;" "I think I had sort of almost a nervous breakdown because I didn't – not really, nobody knew, you know." She suffered a "breakdown" as if she suffocated under the weight of the cloaks. Fran notes that her inability to shed the cloaks was malignant; her silence was "poisonous." Yet at the same time, her silence saved her life.

Speaking

Based on Fran's sentiments expressed above regarding the trauma of silence, one might expect that her thoughts on speaking and giving voice to her experience would evoke opposing sentiments from her. However, a close listen to Fran's reflections on speaking, particularly regarding the time during and years following the war, revealed a distinct voice of dishonesty, deception, falseness. The language Fran repeatedly chose reflected her sense that whatever she spoke about was almost bogus, concocted, or deceitful: "false;" "I told everybody [falsehoods];" "false identity;" "lie;" "it was a very good way to say [something that wasn't true about me];" "sounded false;" "I was hearing myself talking. What's wrong with you?" "stolen memories;" "whatever I would say I felt would not totally be the truth."

*Fran's v*oice of "Speaking"

SPEAKING
• And so I did start to talk about the war but at the same time I would still say that, you know, I was French and it all sounded, it sounded false, you know. • I always told everybody I was, uh, French, born in Corsica, and you know, brought up Catholic and now an atheist. And you know, and I don't know why I did that. • At some point I decided—I realized it's really a false identity.

- Well, it was a lie. I mean, I'm born in Italy of Czech parents.
- I mean, nobody understood… so it was very good for me to say, well I was, you know, I'm French, an ex-Catholic, Protestant, whatever it is, it was just a way not to, uh, to face all this confusion.
- I think part of it was also that I realized in an intimate kind of relationship it all sounded false.
- I had trouble with my personal life and I really didn't know what- and here I was hearing myself talking. What's wrong with you?
- But you see, in a way, I hate to say that, but in a way a lot of these memories are like, uh, stolen memories. Because they're not really—you know, I'm not totally connected to this, and I can't, because I remember one time. And we're speaking in the school, and it's OK, I say this… which has also been helpful in getting me to reconnect emotionally.
- So I say, yeah, I was there during the war. I don't want to—to deny it, you know.
- [I am curious about why you thought you had nothing to say.] Well, because whatever I would say I felt would not be totally the truth, you know. I mean, I could tell them about my adoptive parents but they died and they were old, they were not really my parents. I was stealing my adoptive mother's fame and her identity so I was inauthentic in that way too. My grandparents I don't even know what happened. They were all murdered. I never knew their names….

Given Fran's trauma of having her identity covered over and eclipsed, her language begins to make sense. If she no longer knows who she is, then speaking would reveal her as a phony. This language not only reveals Fran's sense of herself as a phony, it also reflects Fran's feelings of shame. This shame highlights the interpersonal reverberations speaking has for Fran. Of course, speaking is in itself an interpersonal endeavor, but Fran drew attention to the importance of the "other's" perceptions by reflecting on how her verbal assertions would have been perceived by others. Fran understands speaking as asserting one's identity, a task that had become impossible to do without feeling false. Indeed, Fran reveals that she invalidated her identity as soon as she "hear[d] [her]self talking." This pattern of invalidation or negation after assertion of self is reflected in many of her I-poems, two of which are shared below:

I love
I worked
I have
I give
I do
I do

I think
I was
I just

I don't know
I wouldn't
I no way
I never
--
I felt
I was
I managed

I spoke
I spoke
I thought
I thought

I've never

I started
I started

I've never
I have never

As Fran gave voice to both silence and speaking, she revealed her double-bind: to remain silent is to become contaminated and crushed by imposed identities ("breakdown;" "poisoned"), yet to speak is to reveal that she is not true or real, but a phony ("a lie"). To speak while cloaked in imposed identities would have invalidated Fran as a person.

Speaking out, even as an authentic Jewish girl, was never an option for Fran. She had learned the terrifying lesson as a child that to do so was a death sentence.

> I had started to go to school. I think I was six by then. And the Germans had come…and the teacher asked who is, uh, um, Jewish in the class. And I was with my little friend who was Jewish and she raised her hand. And for some bizarre reason I decided not to… There was instinct of preservation…But I did not raise my hand. And two days later my little friend was deported with her family.

There was no way out for Fran. Silence and speaking were both mortally dangerous.

Lifelong Struggle

Fran's struggle to define herself, to bring cohesion to her identity, and to find meaning in her life has been lifelong, and this struggle pervaded every aspect of this interview. In fact, in the time she spent giving this interview, she used the term "I mean" with striking regularity (more than 65 times), which mirrored her desire to literally affirm her identity and find meaning in herself. While the pairs have been taken out of chronological order, here is a poem that matches each of her "I mean" statements with the I-statement that occurs immediately following "I mean":

I mean-I'm trying
I mean-I-I remember
I mean -I started
I mean-I became
I mean -I feel
I mean-I think
I mean-I could tell

Fran's assertions of self-meaning ("I mean") were followed by actions ("trying," "remember," "started"), which led to "feel[ing"] and "tell[ing]." Acting is an affirming process that solidifies her identity and keeps her from suffocating under the weight of the cloaks she has worn.

Reactions and Responses

The interpersonal nature of speaking one's story is salient throughout this interview with Fran. The shame she felt in talking was intensified as she felt victim to the reactions of other people. Fran described how listeners' reactions to her sharing impacted her: "You know, either people feel very sorry or they say who wants to hear about it or… you know. There was always this sense of discomfort… And the shame, also. Yeah, it was an avoidance. I think I would say it was an avoidance." Here Fran suggested that neither reaction- feeling sorry for her or silencing her- makes her feel listened to or validated. Rather, these reactions only magnify Fran's shame. She told of one reaction to an instance when she spoke about her past: "I mean it's difficult because if you say, you know, to somebody or you know, 'I was a child during the war, a Holocaust survivor' they… tell me, 'you look so normal.'" Just under the surface of such a comment is the implication that Fran is not normal, but damaged and strange. Fran has indicated that talking is a way of asserting one's identity, but the listener's reflection back suggests a suspicion of inauthenticity (implying, you don't look like who you say you are). This response mirrors the trauma that Fran experienced in having her identity shrouded. Thus, the listener's reflection further victimizes Fran, adding to her feelings of shame. This shame, as Fran has advised, promoted avoidance and bred silence.

Fran expressed anger about the reactions of others, which often made her feel victimized. She shared a story about a time when she spoke to a group of students and had an experience of unlocking a repressed memory, which terrified her and caused her to abruptly end the talk. She described her anger at the school's reaction (essentially clearing out the students and asking her to leave): "I was furious afterwards. Because it really wasn't nice. The way they handled it. Well, they handled it to protect themselves. They really didn't care what they did to me." Fran's experience is minimized and disregarded in the service of others: the story of her trauma.

Fran's use of the word "it" when referring to her story of trauma ("what it would do to them," "it terrified me," "the way they handle it") also makes an interesting statement about how she herself handles the trauma. The use of the word "it" serves to objectify the experience, creating distance between Fran and the trauma. Instead of referring to "my story," Fran spoke about her history as a separate entity without ownership, not an autobiographical story rooted in her identity. This "it" is seemingly alien to her, what with its destructive power independent of Fran's volition ("what it would do," "it terrified," "they handled it"). This use of "it," reveals both her lack of personal connection to the experience and the powerlessness she feels.

Fran referred to the problematic reactions of others multiple times in the interview. She explained:

> When I speak about this in some of these places, you know, either- as I say- either I get this thing over 'you're so admirable,' which I feel nothing. It's all so bullshit I would say. I don't wanna… I just want to be part of… the problem when you speak is that some people feel they don't have to deal with you or they just, um, you know. I remember one of the places where I spoke. One of the priests came to me and said, 'I'm so honored that I heard you speak.' And then he left. Well, you know. Who cares, you know? I'm too sensitive. That's who I am. There's a way of speaking and a way of responding. I think the 'other' has a very important part.

Her assertion that "it's bullshit" harkens back to her feelings of inauthenticity, as if her listener's reaction is fraudulent. While she has claimed speaking has "been helpful in getting me to reconnect emotionally," being admired by the listener leaves her emotionless ("I feel nothing"). She explained, "the problem when you speak is that some people feel they don't have to deal with you." Admiring Fran for speaking does not make her feel heard or properly "dealt with," but rather dismissed. Similarly, the priest who was honored by Fran's presence subsequently "left," apparently upsetting her by his departure.

Fran had said that the imperative in speaking is "to try to have a story but to tell it in a way that other people can hear it. It's a connection to other people. It has to be a connection to other people." The admiration and praise, rather than making her feel validated, makes her feel dismissed, disregarded, unheard and disconnected. She does not feel authentically recognized. This reiterates the connection between speaking and feeling like a fraud for Fran, highlighting her identity struggles.

Fran has come to be very careful in choosing to whom she discloses, based largely on her gauge of the anticipated response of the listener. It is as if she pre-emptively goes into hiding around individuals she senses will not respond optimally. She explained, "who wants to hear about it? You know. I can find who is interested and who is not." She is looking for listeners who "want" to hear; those who demonstrate their "interest" are different from those who comment to her, then walk away.

Fran opined:

> What's the optimum response? I'm asking myself this. Well, you know, just to, you know, just to see there's a part of my life, you know… to want to talk- it's hard to say. It's like somebody who empathized but does not put you down, you know? That's, uh, not afraid to talk and then goes on talking about something else, you know? That does not get stuck on it. Or who starts to talk about something else… that you feel you can have a coherent discussion… to have a discussion that really has meat in it. Or just say 'I'm glad you're around' or something like this. That something makes you feel you're accepted and [that's part of who you are].

A close listen to Fran's language ("want to talk," "hard to say," "not afraid to talk," "goes on talking," "not get stuck," "have a discussion," "just say"), suggests that Fran values an ease and fluidity in speaking. Fran's desire seemed to be to have other people recognize her past as a part of her, but not the defining component of her identity. In her imagined ideal response, there is no expression of sympathy, no glorification of her heroism, no shocked disbelief. There is simply an acknowledgement and acceptance. Fran expressed gratitude for such a reaction in her recollection of a past encounter: "To just mention it—to be able to mention it in, you know, the usual context, would just, you know, I talked to somebody and they said, 'oh yes you mean the war' and I said, 'yes' and I felt he understood and that was it. And I felt relieved. Because I could be me. I didn't feel I was in hiding."

Making Meaning

Fran repeatedly returned to the expectation that she will reclaim her lost identity by creating a cohesive narrative. In multiple ways, she expressed her desire to find meaning in her life and tell her story as best she can. In so doing, she might make sense of "all this confusion. I realized I had to try to come to terms with that past." Fran is focused on the power of speaking about her experience: "I want to write a story I remember, you know, important pieces;" "I always wanted to find a way to integrate it;" "I mean right now I'm trying to write my story. I fact you're coming at the right time because I remember more because I'm trying to write my story."

Fran explained:

> I tried to reach out to people who would help me, you know, like, remember, reconnect… to reconnect emotionally, because—I tried to reconnect to the fact that I was, uh, that I had gone through the war, but it still didn't mean much emotionally. I mean, there was a real sense of being cut off or not having an emotional connection. And… so when I met my uncle in the 70s… it was wonderful because suddenly, you know, my mother became a real person… I mean told me the whole story, and that's what really brought me back to a sense of myself.

Fran's reference to her mother as a "real person" stands in stark contrast to her earlier accounts of having nothing but "false" and "stolen" pieces of an identity. Finding connections to her life before the war, her old identity before it was shrouded, has been key to rediscovering "a sense of myself." Speaking, for Fran, is aimed at building "a connection to other people."

Talking built bridges to her past, allowing Fran to "reconnect" with the parts of her that had been "forgotten" in the covering over of her identity. In the process of rediscovering herself, Fran began to cast off the cloaks that had obscured her, as evidenced by her language. She explained, "But this time I decided I'm going to tell people. I can't deal with [9/11] because of my background. And it was such a relief ...that takes away the sense of shame." For Fran, talking is "relief" that "takes away the sense of shame." This unburdening is heard in other language Fran used to describe the benefits of talking: "this past had such an effect on me effectively that the only way to get rid of it is to say something. And then I'm more free to be in the present." There is a sense of catharsis in this language as she is able to "get rid" of the trauma by talking about it; that venting "takes away" the negative feelings about the trauma.

Fran reflected why she was not focused on creating a cohesive narrative sooner: "I had so much to try to deal with the present that, uh, I should have to deal much later. You know. That it sort of may have superseded any other... you know, trying to put myself together." The language of burden is evident in her explanation; Fran had to "deal" with the layers of identity that had been placed on her in hiding. "I mean there were so many issues always involved and I think, uh, I think also I was trying so hard to adapt ... It took so much energy." Fran's effort to adapt meant carrying the weight of her cloaks. She had no energy for reconnection with the past.

Now that Fran has begun the process of unburdening herself, she has rediscovered "this sense of self-pride." Fran remembered one of the first times she was able to proudly assert her identity: "yes, I am [Jewish]." The empowerment and integration Fran has found in speaking is reflected in an I-poem:

I just feel
I mean

I talked
I said

I felt
I felt
I could

Trauma and Healing

When she was six years old, Fran learned that to speak about her true identity as a Jewish girl meant certain death. She was placed into hiding. For Fran, being in hiding meant being cloaked in lies; predetermined scripts written by strangers who determined who she was. This stripping and obscuring of her identity is Fran's most salient trauma, which caused her to forget who she was. She was left her feeling uncertain and fraudulent. Fran's uncertainty served to silence her: how can she speak if speaking declared her identity, yet she no longer knew who she was? To speak would have been to express the voice of an imposter. Fran felt like a phony, disguised in other's expectations, images, and religions. Fran was in a no-win situation with no way out, and this enraged her. Fran had lost her true, authentic voice. Slowly, Fran began to find the threads back to connect her to who she was before she was stripped and disguised. This connection has enabled her to speak, and in speaking, she unburdens herself from the layers of lies that have enshrouded her.

Having found his song, the song of self-sufficiency, fully resurrected, cleansed and given breath, free from any encumbrance other than the workings of his own heart and the bonds of the flesh, having accepted the responsibility for his own presence in the world, he is free to soar above the environs that weighed and pushed his spirit into terrifying contractions. –stage direction, August Wilson, "Joe Turner's Come and Gone"

Reva

Joy and woe are woven fine. –William Blake

The only true paradise is a paradise lost. –Marcel Proust

I was nervous to call Reva until she answered the phone. She immediately recognized my name and invited me to her home for an interview. I didn't want to show up empty-handed since she'd been so accommodating in scheduling the meeting and had invited me into her home, so I brought her flowers. When the elevator door opened to her floor, Reva was there, awaiting my arrival. Her face brightened when she saw me, and she extended her hand, noticing the flowers. She exclaimed, "Aren't you sweet! You didn't have to do that!" She invited me into her apartment, unwrapping the flowers immediately and cutting the stems to put them in a vase of water. As she prepared the arrangement, she gave me a tip: if you put a spoonful of sugar or a sugar cube in the water for the flowers, they will perk right up. She poured a little sugar in the water before offering me cookies and tea.

I immediately felt at home in Reva's presence; she was vibrant and beautiful, with smooth ivory skin and bobbed white hair. She seemed youthful, yet she exuded a motherly, welcoming, warm aura. She prepared a plate of cookies and arranged the chairs in her living room so that we could sit close, face-to-face. Reva's hardwood-floored living room seemed bare, and the lighting was sparse. She turned on one lamp in the room as it was getting dark. Reva's living room did not have a couch or a coffee table or a television; instead there was simply a desk (on which a laptop sat, turned on), an armchair (where she sat), a kitchen chair (pulled from the desk), and the stool on which we placed the tape recorder. We were the only two in her quiet apartment.

The place seemed devoid of life, which stood in contrast to Reva's lively nature. When she began to speak, her voice seemed to echo, bouncing off the bare floor and largely bare walls. It pierced through the silence of the evening and began to fill the room with live energy. As Reva spoke, I tried to take her in, but it was almost too much for me at times. She seemed strong, certain, connected to herself, psychologically-minded, articulate, likeable, and so full of emotion that her energy was almost tangible. It was contagious, and she was so open that I instinctively reacted by backing away several times during our interview. In retrospect, I wish I had stayed with her at her most open and vulnerable; I do not know why I backed away. I had the distinct feeling throughout the entirety of our two-hour meeting that I was thrilled. Not terrified or elated, simply thrilled. I left her home full of energy.

Who Is She?

As the threat of the Nazis grew in Poland, Reva's mother and father grew fearful, and the decision was made to place Reva into hiding deep in the Poland forest. She was left in the care of a forest watchman and his family, where her mother believed she would be safe and well cared for, but where she was traumatized. Reva was young- a mere four years old- when she was sent to the forest, and she remained there for over a year until her mother and father were liberated from a concentration camp. She explains this in the first person voice, owning the experience with her use of the word "I":

> I was abandoned. I was abandoned and then I was put in a place in the middle of the forest with this forest watchman and a woman who had a child my age, who was, uh, very superstitious, always scared the living daylights out of me predicting that the house would burn down and I would break a leg and they didn't relate to me the way one relates to a child. I was there, but I was not, I spent most of my time alone, almost all my time alone. I was four and five and uh, there was a man who was a forest watchman who though I know from my mother's account that he liked me and he was very courageous, he took me in when it threatened the survival of his own family. But, no one ever talked to me. Not him either. And he always walked around with a gun, and boots, and a military uniform, and he was a very frightening figure. And I always was frightened of him and I was just squelched there. You know suddenly I am with these strangers in this hut in the middle of nowhere. In the middle of the forest where I was alone. In the warm weather I spent all of my time alone in the forest. So, I was enraged at the whole thing.

Throughout the interview, Reva returned to the horror of her experience, explaining her trauma. Each time she revisited her experience in the forest, she recalled additional details that paint the picture of the trauma. In the passage below, however, she drove home the experiences as she imposed them on the listener, using the word "you" instead of "I." In so doing, Reva encouraged the listener to imagine—in a very personal way—what the experience must have felt like. Perhaps this was her attempt to enhance one's understanding of and empathy for her trauma:

> It's very hard to understand on an emotional level to be four and five, and to be alone in the world. To be, to have been raised in a middle class environment and to be in the middle of a forest with peasants and who don't give a hoot about you and who, the physical stuff is also very bad. There was no plumbing, there was no electricity, there was, uh, very little food, there was you never took a bath. Everything was just filled with worms and lice and nits, it was, it doesn't look that way on the pictures, but most of the time it was a horrid disgusting-filled life. And you felt very uncared for. You were very uncared for. And you were alone. And it is a devastating thing for a child to be alone like that.

She returned again to the experience, as if she needed to ensure she was communicating the degree of pain inflicted by the atrocity:

> I was four when I was taken away, I was alone in the world at four and it these people didn't relate to me and I was alone always in the forest and no one talked to me for two years. And I was terrified of the woman who was predicting disaster all of the time and the man, who was gone a lot of the time he was patrolling the forest but when he would come back with little animals… It was all really brutal for a little child like that. I felt just brutalized. And I was alone. And I was completely alone. I didn't think I would see my parents ever again.

As if her experience were not horrific enough, Reva added later that she feared for her life. She recalled being constantly under the threat of death in the forest:

> The people who had me, uh, the family of the man who kept me, were putting tremendous pressure on him to kill me. Because Christians were being killed, those who were harboring Jews, that he was putting the family, and his fiancée's family in grave danger. In grave danger, to keep me. But he didn't do it, obviously. But still, I knew, they talked in front of me about it.

Reva struggled with resentment and anger at her mother, both for leaving her in the forest, and for taking her away from a place that she had become connected to:

> My mother came for me. And I went with her. But I lost something too because the forest were my parents, the trees. And then I lost my forest. And I was very damaged by then, by that time. And I didn't really relate to my parents very well.

After the war, Reva and her family wandered through several cities in an attempt to rebuild some sort of normalcy, and finally ended up in New York state, where some members of her family lived. Her father, a physician, went about setting up a practice, and her mother gave birth to Reva's little brother. However, her brother had "problems" due to what Reva believes was her mother's malnutrition in the concentration camp. She assumed the caretaker role for her brother and her parents and brother:

> I saw that my parents were extremely anxious… I saw that they were just terribly anxious and I was very upset in that house because, it was such an unexpressed feeling of sorrow… there was a feeling of misery, of unhappiness at home.

Eventually, when she was sixteen, Reva moved away from home to live with a cousin in New York City ("I never went home again. I just little went home for little visits but I never went home again."). She endured a string of bad marriages, ("I was not a social person. I was married, I was afraid to be alone, I was married four times,") unfulfilling attempts at therapy, ("I started at nineteen and I went to lots of different therapists, and it was just talk.... I didn't get anywhere because I was so disconnected that talking didn't do anything for me"), and eventually gave birth to two sons. Recently, Reva helped publish a memoir that her mother had composed after the war and stored in a closet for decades.

Despite her suffering and failed therapy in the past, Reva reported that she finally has recently begun recovery from her trauma, in the form of connection to her feelings ("Yes. I feel much more connected"). When asked how her life has changed since infusing feelings into her life, Reva responded:

> It is much, much better. Now I have relationships with friends that love me and that I care for. My relationship with my husband is much better than it has ever been. Um, I feel, I feel better. And I hope, that after I finish doing promoting on [my mother's] book, that I want to go back to my painting, and that will also be better. More authentic.

On the surface, it sounds like Reva's life has begun to improve as she copes with her past trauma and recovers feeling that was once lost.

Dissociation

Reva's history, according to her factual recounting of the events during and since the Holocaust, seems straightforward: she was hidden, abandoned and alone, in the forest under the "care" of a brutal forest watchman and his family. She has spent her life dealing with this trauma and all of its repercussions. She retells this traumatic experience again and again, as if she cannot find words brutal enough to capture the horror, as if she needs to convince the listener of the atrocity of it all. Yet, at the same time, she told a very different story of this same traumatic experience: one of life and connection and utopia. In fact, throughout her narrative, stunning contradictions arose as two distinct and opposite voices tell the same stories. These dual stories are of the trauma/bliss of the forest, of her driving desire/aversion for connection with her experience and with others, of her rich and intense/dull and disconnected emotional life. These are not allegories, with one story over top another story; the second stories are not covered or unknown or beneath the first. Rather, each exist in parallel, side by side with its opposite. I am overwhelmed by Reva's narrative, as the contradictions assault my sense of logic and tendencies to categorize and dichotomize.

Dissociation is considered one of the hallmarks in the diagnosis of Post Traumatic Stress Disorder (PTSD). In psychiatric terms, dissociation is defined as "a psychological defense mechanism in which specific, anxiety-provoking thoughts, emotions, or physical sensations are separated from the rest of the psyche" (retrieved from: http://education.yahoo.com/reference/dictionary/entry/ dissociation). In the case of trauma survivors, the dissociated part usually consists of the thoughts and emotions associated with the traumatic event. Indeed, Reva explained that she experiences dissociation in this sense: "My defense was to sort of to go, um, uh, to sort of be, um, not really in the present, kind of, um, out of it. Really out of it. I mean I was really, really out of it."

In listening to her description, one learns that Reva cut off her experience from the rest of her psyche, resulting in an "out of it" state. Again and again, she told of her split: "I was very dissociated," "Because I was somewhere else," "I was just, just out of it," "I don't even know if I even thought about it, I was just completely out of it," "It was too painful to actually experience it as it was happening," "I didn't really get connected to my emotions," "I felt very dissociated from my feelings," "I was like flying," "So I think I was, uh, cut off from my feelings," "I was also so out of it," "I did not feel my impulses. I didn't feel anything from the inside. I was really completely detached." This disconnect between her feelings and the rest of her psyche, while repeatedly described by Reva, was not consistently clear. As she described her experience in the forest, she used language revealing the intense emotion she felt during her trauma.

Contrapuntal Voices

This becomes evident as the varied voices Reva gives to her experience are lined up together to illuminate the stark contrast between them. Reva was able to consciously access and talk about her emotions, while at the same time, denying that they were accessible to her. In the left column is one point, and the corresponding part on the other column is the counterpoint, which is directly contradictory. Often, Reva made each of these opposite points in the same breath, in the same sentence.

Reva's "Emotionless" voice vs. "Emotion-Filled" voice

EMOTIONLESS	EMOTION-FILLED
• I was very dissociated • My defense was to sort of …be, um, not really in the present, kind of, um, out of it. Really out of it. I mean I was really, really out of it. • Because I was somewhere else • I was just, just out of it • I don't even know if I even thought about it, I was just completely out of it • It was too painful to actually experience it as it was happening • I didn't really get connected to my emotions • I felt very dissociated from my feelings • I was like flying • So I think I was, uh, cut off from my feelings • I was also so out of it. • I did not feel my impulses. I didn't feel anything from the inside. I was really completely detached.	• I remember when I was a real sentient being • I always was frightened • I was enraged • I was terrified • I felt just brutalized • I was very angry • I was very, uh, frightened • I was afraid • I was very, very fragile, very frightened I remember being angry at my mother. Being very angry at my mother, but very much in love with my father. • I just loved him very much • They knew how disturbed I was, how distraught I was. • I was very angry at them, but I also felt terrible guilt. • I couldn't even restrain the anger you know I was furious for a long time, I made my mother cry daily because I was so angry.

Indeed, Reva had access to that which she claimed to have disconnected or unable to feel. While there was an obvious and distinct split between two voices outlined above, this split in her psyche is vertical rather than horizontal. In other words, she could access and speak from both voices, rather than submerging a part of herself in her unconscious. In this way, Reva's voices provide evidence of dissociation rather than repression, as they exist side by side and share approximately equal proportions of Reva's narrative. Repeatedly, she made contradictory statements, with affirmation and negation appearing in succession, suggesting a frequent switch between two accessible experiences: "I was there/I was not," "I wasn't/I was," "I don't want/I want, "I do/I don't," "I could/I can't."

While Reva was aware of both states of being, she has not connected them or reconciled the competing messages. Reva did not seem bothered by or attentive to the contradiction and made no attempt to explain the mismatch, providing evidence of two conscious experiences, which Freud termed "double consciousness" (Herman, 1992). This lack of cohesion in her narrative consistently arose. Astoundingly, even when discussing what she had repeatedly presented as the horrific Holocaust trauma, she presented an image of absolute utopia alongside the atrocity. She spoke of the forest as preventing feeling, stifling her into a state that sounded much like death, traumatizing her. At the same time, in the opposite column, a voice described the forest as a life-giving force that promoted emotional intensity and ecstasy that Reva has been chasing ever since the trauma:

Reva's voice of "Forest was Traumatizing" vs. "Forest was Invigorating"

Forest Prevented Feeling- TRAUMATIZING	Forest Promoted Feeling – INVIGORATING
• You know being a child in that forest and knowing that my life was in the balance all the time, and that I had to please at any cost, you know, I could never express, I couldn't cry, I couldn't criticize. I had to, I was like squeezed into being a flat person, without responses, without emotions. • I lived in paradise half of the time, but it wasn't real paradise, it was a hallucination. I was running away from horror.	• Because I always remember what it was like to be in that forest. I always remember what I felt like when I looked at the sky and those stars, when I was really connected to the universe. That it was so exalting, it was what life is about. And it doesn't pay to be alive if you don't have that. • I had those feelings. Those feelings of paradise. It was like paradise. Bliss. Perfect bliss. And every once in awhile I have a minute of it. Its like, you think, oh my goodness, just achieving that, is worth living for. • Maybe I can still recapture that

• I remember just one thing: that I did not feel my impulses. I didn't feel anything from the inside. I was really completely detached. • It was the most awful time …	capacity to experience that, that keen sense of perception. • I remember when I was a real sentient being as a little girl in the forest. I responded to nature with all my might and the beauty of it, I was so open to it and I was connected to the universe through that forest. I think it was a high point in my life. …I can't say wonderful but it was intense. So, I would like to get some of that back. That was incredible. • I want it back. I had a sense of color, too. It was just magic. Just absolute magic.

In the left column, Reva explained that her time in the forest robbed her of feeling, leaving her emotionally dead. Her language ("squeezed into being a flat person, without responses, without emotions," "running away from horror," "detached,") when coupled with her description from the left column of the previous voices, ("awful," "too painful," "cut off"), reflects the violation and violence inflicted by this traumatizing event. She sounded tortured.

At the same time, Reva described her time in the forest as the absolute essence of life. She described her experience in a very different, vibrant voice: "it doesn't pay to be alive if you don't have that," "feelings," "paradise," "perfect bliss," "worth living for," "keen sense of perception," "real sentient being," "all my might," "beauty," "connected," "color," "open," "high point," "intense," "incredible," "magic. Just absolute magic." She sounds euphoric, bursting with emotion. Her language sounds orgasmic, mirroring the life-giving moment of reproduction, when birth becomes possible.

Just as Reva described the life-taking torture of her traumatic experience, she also describes the life-giving essence of the exact same experience. Just as she claimed that she endured a horribly painful and horrific torture, she identified her own emotional climax, a feeling that she has spent her whole life since searching for. How can this be?

Throughout her narrative, Reva repeatedly matched denial with assertion with almost mathematic precision. The proportions of each were perfectly matched, to the point where one can predict what she will say next as she cycled through the affirmation and negation. Her I-statements, in order, follow her psyche as it exacts with precision the shifting pattern between two voices:

I
I experienced
I went
I was

I don't
I don't

I went
I went

I didn't
I didn't

I was
I guess
I must

I don't know
I wasn't

Each negative was followed with a positive, and vice/versa. Each crescendo of feeling matched perfectly with the dimuendo, suggesting that Reva backs away each time she gets too close to her emotions. Indeed, this apparent need for escape from emotional knowledge occurred repeatedly. Reva struggled with feeling what she feels:

I would
I've had
I believe
I feel
I'm
I get there
I feel

I mean
I am afraid

Each feeling, merging emotion with experience, was met with fear. Reva's I-poems revealed her apparent desire to feel, but the feeling was followed by the negation, here in the form of fear, which shut down the emotion. And thus, the cycle begins again.

I went
I submitted
I was
I was
I remember

I didn't feel anything
I was really completely detached

The connection to the events, via memories, thoughts and feelings, was repeatedly avoided and denied. Reva continually stated, then avoided; asserted, then denied. This pattern, repeated, suggests that the connection to feelings is threatening. Similarly, Reva's connections to others seemed dangerous, burdensome, and stifling:

I feel very burdened
I don't want
I don't want
I want

I want freedom
I
I just want freedom to breathe

Reva seemed to communicate that she shuts down strong emotional connection to others. Reva appeared to be attempting to cope with, manage, and work through the trauma as she reiteratively cycled through her thoughts and feelings, voicing her emotional, connected, knowing side, though only fleetingly. Her silencing, denying, negating voice consistently surfaced, causing Reva to assert that she doesn't know, doesn't think, and doesn't feel.

Coping with Trauma

When reflecting on her traumatic Holocaust experience, Reva expressed:

I'm amazed
I survived it

Yet throughout her narrative, Reva explicitly explained how she was able to survive: to "check out" of reality, and to "check in" to a fantasy world she created in the forest, where the forest creatures were her friends and the trees were her parents. While she believes this saved her life, ("If I hadn't [checked out], I wouldn't have been able to live through it. That kept me alive"), Reva offered a very different recommendation for others enduring trauma. In fact, while she claimed to have "checked back in" to life, and in doing so, healing her wounds and dealing with her trauma ("Oh, yes! I am very happy about [checking in]. Better late than never"), a different reality appeared in her narrative.

Again, she spoke in two distinct voices as she responded to the question: "Is it better to express or avoid your trauma?" The left column below represents "advice": speaking not in personal terms, but rather advising an ambiguous "you," this column is full of "should's." It provides a very clear answer to the question: expression is the key to recovery. On the other hand, Reva responded to the question in a very different way in the right column, revealing her own reality, clearly in the first person "I." Reva's coping mechanisms consist entirely of avoidance: avoidance of emotion, avoidance of connection to her experiences and to others, and the desire to avoid expression.

Reva's voice of "Advice" vs. voice of "Reality"

ADVICE	REALITY
• Well checking out means you have no life. You're living nowhere. You're nowhere. You're not experiencing what's around you, you can't have any close relationships, you have nothing. You have to check back in.	• [If I hadn't checked out], I wouldn't have been able to live through it. That kept me alive. • I don't want to be a caretaker anymore and I don't want to, you know what I want? I want freedom. In lots of ways. Emotionally, physically… freedom from painful entanglement with my kids, I, I just want freedom to breathe. • I don't want any re-involvement with me in terms of, whatever. I want them to focus on their life.
• I would say tell people. You know, when you don't talk about it,… you become a stranger to yourself. People will see you as someone you're not. …You come off as just, just like the next person, you're just one of the guys. One of the gals. And you, you live in a false world, and since you're hidden, you are a stranger to yourself. I think you have to talk about it a lot with people that you really trust. And talk about it, and not just talk about it, but identify yourself with it. You *are* that, you know. Whatever your experience is, you *are* that. And it lives with you forever and if you want to be a sane person, you incorporate that, and you are that. Because otherwise you are cheating yourself in	• …which I did for most of my life, • … And maybe that's what I wanted for awhile. • No. And I did not. No, and I don't want to talk about my experience with them. And I never did. And even now, I don't think I, I mean I wrote a little bit of the book but I never could express it with my parents, I don't know why. There was a kind of shame about it, or…. Umm, I can't even explain the feeling. I couldn't open myself up with them that much. • No. No. Never spoke with him • No. I don't talk to them. • No, we don't talk much about it. He's involved with his own life. • No, sometimes he would ask me things, or, but uh, I don't like to talk

your life, of your life. You can't be a whole person and deny a part of yourself. Or, or especially a formative experience like that. And it's going to color your life. It's gonna color your thoughts and your opinions and you think, okay, it's going to make you fearful, pessimistic or other things, and that's not valid. But it is valid. It's as valid as someone else's opinion who had a nice, lovely life and a you know, and thinks everything is hunky-dorey. It's just as valid and its just as real an expression of what exists and uh, I think it's very valuable. You have to believe that your experience is valid and important and not hide it.	about it with the kids. • Maybe I don't like to talk about it, actually. Uh, because I don't want, I don't feel that they can ever understand what really happened, and I don't feel I can ever in words explain it to them, and it seems like, uh, it's not going to bear fruit, this topic with them. And then I don't want them to, I don't know, get, uh, wrong ideas about things. I don't know, I just, if they don't ask, I don't go there. • Oh, everybody knows, but they never talk about it with me. • Yes. I do [prefer not to talk about it with my kids]. Because I don't really think I could ever really explain.
• And I believe that feelings are physical energy. And if they are not expressed, they are lodged in the musculature.	• I can't envision myself having talked to them, nor do I want to. I think that first of all it would be painful for them. And then, I don't think they want, I don't think I want them to know me that that way. That much, that deeply.
• They'd rather not know. So that's like an ostrich putting his head in the sand. • If you're angry, but if you're crying you're encouraged to keep on crying –whatever it is you feel, you feel it there and its marvelous. It goes very quickly. It really gets to your issues… It's very healthy.	• And I hid it, most of my life. • And for awhile, uh, no I didn't speak about it to anybody but sometimes, you know it would come out, but I, I, I hid it mostly. But you know I was very, uh, frightened. I was not a social person. • I guess one can repress to such an extent that just cuts it completely off. And then you, you know, you, I suppose you could survive that way.
• But maybe it isn't a waste. Maybe it just takes such a long time to work through things, maybe they had a part in helping me to work through it.	• Because I wasted time and I wasted a lot of money.
• But you see, my friend said that too. She said when she was about eighteen or nineteen and you'd ask her about her life, she'd say, "Oh, everything's fine." And then about twenty she	• I think there was a lot of numbness and then with a little bit of safety, the horror really came home and I think they were quite, quite upset for many years afterwards, reliving all of this stuff.

completely, like, broke down and couldn't function. • And I, and my friend and I, we say, we talk about it, we say, how can she, after what she went through, having never been in therapy, how can she go on, you know, this way?	• I remember that night, my father wanted to tell them what happened to their relatives and they stopped him, they didn't want to hear it, it was much too painful to listen to it.
• Well, I don't know her that well. I have to rely on my friend talking about her sister but it seems that her relationship with her husband isn't so great, but its all kind of like, everyday stuff. • I would guess, if I think about it, that she is living a very restricted emotional life. • She constricted herself into some sort of a normalistic existence.	• It would take a long time of delving, and I don't know that I want to do that. • I think everybody was aware of it… very morose. Pessimistic and down all the time and suffering. I don't know anyone…divorced from it.

Avoidance of Trauma

In the left column, Reva cautioned "you" that avoidance is harmful. She advised that life is only possible when one is able to connect with others in close relationships. Therefore, the key to life is talking with others, connecting one to others, sharing experiences and emotions. To check out or avoid means to have no life, a point she makes clear in the deadly language she uses to describe avoidance: "you have no life," "you're living nowhere," "you're nowhere," "you're not experiencing," "you can't have close relationships," "you have nothing," "cheating yourself of life," "can't be whole," "lodged in musculature," "putting his head in the sand," "broke down," and "couldn't function." Her imagery captures the deadness and inability to really live when one avoids. Peculiarly, her language in describing avoidance of trauma, "stranger," "false world," "hidden," "constricted," and "restricted," sounds identical to the language

Reva uses when describing the traumatic aspects of her Holocaust forest experience:

- You know suddenly I am with these *strangers* in this hut in the middle of nowhere.
- I *didn't really get connected* to my emotions
- I was like flying
- So I think I was, uh, *cut off from my feelings*
- I was also so *out of it.*
- I did not feel my impulses. *I didn't feel anything* from the inside. *I was really completely detached.*
- You know being a child in that forest and knowing that my life was in the balance all the time, and that I had to please at any cost, you know, I could never express, I couldn't cry, I couldn't criticize. I had to, I was like *squeezed* into being a flat person, without responses, without emotions.
- *It wasn't real* paradise, it was a hallucination.

This parallel suggests that Reva finds avoidance of the experience, thoughts, and emotions as traumatizing as the worst parts of her Holocaust trauma. On the other hand, she asserted that to talk, express, and "identify" that "you are that," is connected to mental health and a sense of self-worth ("sane," "valid," "valuable," "important"). According to the clear merit she placed in expression and the mortal danger she warned of in avoidance, one would predict without hesitation that Reva would be an "expressor."

In the right column, however, Reva's contrapuntal voice speaks for herself, describing and owning through the "I" which path she has chosen. This column reveals quite the opposite of the expressor. In fact, checking out and avoiding her experience, her emotions, and her connection to others is tied directly to life. It enabled her to survive ("That kept me alive"), and will provide her with "freedom to breathe." She asserted that expression is not going to "bear fruit." The life imagery associated here with avoidance directly contradicts the imagery in the opposite column, which associates avoidance with death. In this column, pain and trauma arises only in expression of her experience ("It would take a long time of delving, and I don't know that I want to do that," "very morose. Pessimistic and down all the time and suffering," "too painful to listen to it," "horror really came home," "quite, quite upset," "painful entanglement," "shame," "I couldn't open myself up with them that much," "it would be painful for them. And then, I don't think they want, I don't think I want them to know me that that way. That much, that deeply").

Despite evidence to the contrary, Reva claimed that she has "checked in," expressing her emotions and facing her experience. She was able to clearly communicate to the listener that she favors and enacts avoidance in her own life, but to herself, she seemed to believe that she has taken the advice in the left column. Likewise, in her I-poems, Reva's striving toward expression is evident. However, the I-poems clearly illuminate the lack of progress she makes, again, as an iterative process, one voice shuts down and negates the attempts toward integration of the experience, the emotions, and the connections:

I have
I care
I feel
I feel
I hope
I finish
I want

I don't talk
I am
I am
I don't like
I don't like
I don't want

I don't feel
I don't feel

In her language, "care," "hope," "want," there is a striving towards and desire for connection and feeling, which was negated as strongly as it was desired. It sounds as if Reva wanted to get to a point of connection with the emotion and with others, but she was unable ("I don't"). Reva seeks intense connection and expression, yet finds these things difficult and painful. This vicious cycle plays out in the interview, without progression or improvement. It's as if the trauma comes for Reva, not in avoidance as she asserted in her "Advice" voice, but in the connection and expression of the half of herself that remembers and feels. While her advice is emphatic and appeals to the age-old common psychic wisdom, she is unable to take it.

For Reva, dissociation is evidenced by two experiences coexisting, unreconciled. She did not attempt to explain the contradictions in her narrative—in fact, she didn't even seem to hear them. However, the two voices do not reflect different levels of consciousness; they appear side-by side, sometimes in the same breath. One part of Reva is not dissociated from the whole; instead, the two voices of Reva are split from each other, but easily accessible.

Similarly, contradictions were evident in Reva's explanation of coping. While she advised that it is best to talk and express extensively in order to become connected to oneself and "real," she does not take her own advice. Instead, she explained why silence and avoidance has been necessary for her, and how she has used it throughout her life since the Holocaust. Reva cycled through this struggle with talking, knowing, and feeling, which was repeatedly shut down in a voice that silences, avoids, and disconnects from others and emotions.

Trauma and Healing

For Reva, as for all hidden children, survival depended on her ability to remain silent and invisible. Reva's her time in the forest required that she not be an imposition on the watchman or his family, and she had to split off her needs, her emotions, and any features that distinguished her as a human being:

> You know being a child in that forest and knowing that my life was in the balance all the time, and that I had to please at any cost, you know, I could never express, I couldn't cry, I couldn't criticize. I had to, I was like squeezed into being a flat person, without responses, without emotions.

This split in Reva's psyche is the hallmark of her trauma. It is consistently evidenced in her narrative by her diametrically opposed contradictory statements: the trauma/bliss of the forest, her driving desire/aversion for connection with others, her intense/dull emotional life, her belief that expression/avoidance heals trauma. Reva's trauma as a hidden child, of being "squeezed into a flat person" and silenced, has left her of two minds. While these two notions seem completely at odds and baffling, Reva never seemed confused. To her, it seemed to make perfect sense.

Yvonne

Such mechanisms are analogous to the involuntary grace by which an oyster, coping with an irritating grain of sand, creates a pearl.
–George Vaillant

Yvonne's effusive warmth and extreme optimism were evident from the moment we first spoke. When I telephoned her to ask her for an interview, her response was a joyful and enthusiastic one. "I'd be delighted to," she exclaimed, and then invited me to her home. She insisted that we meet at her home rather than a neutral location, as she opined that we'd be more comfortable, and besides, she said, "I'd love to show you my home." Yvonne welcomed me in, and I instantly felt comfortable. Yvonne's warm smile and cheerful eyes contributed to a vibrancy, youth, and sprightly demeanor that put me at ease and made me feel like I was the only person in the world.

Yvonne showed me her meticulously clean and tidy studio apartment, taking time to introduce me to her library of carefully catalogued books. She is a teacher through and through, and explained that later that day she was going to teach a French class at a local university. She chose a place to sit, ensuring that I was comfortable and the setting was appropriate for the interview. She paused to admire the view from her window, expressing her appreciation for the beauty of the summer day, for her lovely apartment, and for my visit.

I spent time introducing my project, and concluded with a long statement: "So I'd love to hear your experience about sharing or not sharing and what factors contributed to your silence versus your speaking." Yvonne responded, "Very good. In order to make sense of what happened, I have to begin with the time when the whole world fell apart." She then began to tell me about her life.

During the interview, Yvonne frequently addressed me by my name. This was a simple act, yet striking; it was an instant jolt every time I heard it. It was a personal connection, a recognition of me as an individual and it communicated care. No matter how personal or horrific the memory Yvonne was sharing, she remained incredibly attuned to the reactions and comfort of her listener. She paused, often at the most intense moments of her story, to see if I needed a tissue, a snack, some tea, or an adjustment to the air conditioning. She took time to find ways to relate to me, asking where I was in birth order compared to my siblings, inquiring how I got the scar on my arm. Yvonne's keen ability to connect with her listener made her shared experience all the more poignant, yet also more digestible. She was a skilled communicator.

Who Is She?

Yvonne was born in 1929, and was followed four years later by a sister. She lived with her sister, paternal grandmother, mother and father, (who were merchants in their own family business), in a Paris suburb. In June 1940, when Yvonne was 10 years old, her mother called her into the house from the garden where she had been playing with her sister. Her mother instructed her to pack her things and get into the car, which she did. Her beloved dog came to the car door as he was accustomed to riding with the family, but Yvonne's mother explained that the dog could not come with them. Yvonne became upset, so her mother said she would ask the neighbor to care for the dog until they returned. Yvonne continued:

> I'm watching this, you know. And I remember the moment as though it was right now. I'm watching this, and I see her. She's talking to the guy. A little longer than seemed necessary to me, and he's—comes out. He goes back into his house, and he comes out with a shotgun and a rope. And to my horror, he ties the dog to the tree, and the car began to move when I heard the shotgun. He—he couldn't keep her. A big dog…Well, from that moment on, I was only maybe ten and a half? I said to myself, 'I don't know if I will ever—my life is over. I'm just gonna be some crazy kid running around, you know. I won't be able to go back to school. My dog is dead….I don't know. I began to—uh, I couldn't verbalize it for

> you, but I had this absolute clear feeling that from this moment on, it was over. What was before is finished.

Yvonne's family fled to Toulouse without her father, who had been taken away to a work camp. The family was frequently forced to move to different places, sleeping on the streets until they found shelter in a shack out in the country. As the Germans were advancing, Yvonne's mother decided that the safest place for her daughters was in a convent, where there was an orphanage. It was there that Yvonne would spend four years during the war, baptized as "Mary Marguerite." Yvonne's mother was deported and underwent horrific medical experimentation; her father survived brutalization in work and concentration camps. She detailed the horrors of the experience of her family: "I tell you this story, Emily, because it's catastrophe after catastrophe after catastrophe." After the war, Yvonne's family was reunited; her parents, though virtually unrecognizable, had survived their terrible traumas and tracked each other, and their daughters, down.

Yvonne's ability to stay connected to the listener while telling her story, even the most horrific parts, signaled a level of mastery over her trauma. In fact, her interview was characterized by Yvonne's sense of authority, agency, competence, and choice. Her attitude is captured in one of her I-poems:

I know
I've had

I can say
I reclaimed
I got
I changed

I said

I said
I mean

I took
I
I explain
I said
I said

I took
I took

Yvonne's active voice in this poem is filled with a sense of purpose and ability.

Yvonne literally took her trauma and transformed and interpreted it somehow, making meaning and molding it into an impetus for positive growth. She explained that her experience during the war "gave me the opportunity to start something new. You see, I have the ability to change things from a negative to a positive." Yvonne's resilience is reflected in another of her I-poems:

I didn't know
I said
I wasn't
I didn't know
I couldn't
I didn't
I hadn't

I went
I mean
I go up
I know
I know
I make
I make
I have

Here is further evidence of Yvonne's ability to turn negative into positive. She "didn't," "wasn't," "couldn't," but relied on her knowledge; she then "made," and "had." Yvonne shifts the meaning, making herself both incredibly powerful and still conscious of her impact on others.

Speaking

Yvonne's skill at speaking is the result of a lifetime of practice. Since the war, the traumatic experiences of her family have been subjected to remembering, telling, and re-telling. She recounted her parents' tendency to vocalize what happened:

> I heard the stories that they were telling each other and I wouldn't interrupt them, and I would just listen. That's where I get a lot of information. And I mean, later on I had the opportunity to get even more information except my mother didn't want to talk. You know, my dad talked mostly. My mom talked to him but not to us.

Talking was part of the ethos of Yvonne's family, which she observed as an adolescent. Speaking about the Holocaust was commonplace for her parents and the larger Jewish community in which she lived: "people got together with whoever survived and helped each other. There was like a little community. They absolutely [talked about what had happened]. Particularly my father. My father wrote his own memoirs, which I have." While Yvonne's parents talked to each other and their community, her mother in particular took pains to ensure that their children were not directly exposed to the tales of their trauma. Yvonne explained that her mother did not tell her about her suffering: "It was too horrible. I would have done the same as a mother. Now, when I think about it, I wouldn't have told my children. What for? I mean, it was inhuman what happened. Most of what I know I know from my father and from reading." Yvonne understood that her mother was indeed speaking about what happened to her, but also strove to protect Yvonne from the details.

As an adult, Yvonne first shared her experiences as a hidden child at a meeting of Holocaust survivors. Expression, by then a familiar family practice with regards to the trauma of the war, seemed to come easily and naturally for her:

> I told my story—I was not the only one in the room who had been a hidden child. I was not. And that was a revelation for me to have found that there were other people like me. [Was it difficult?] No. No. Not at all. Because by then I trusted them. You know what it is? It's a matter of trust. If I'm in a situation where I do not feel that kind of connection that I have with you, for instance, then I don't [tell]. I just go through the motions.

Yvonne stressed the importance of connection with another individual as a crucial element in speaking out about her experience. Yvonne describes the "revelation" of not being alone in her experience, but the vital ingredient is not necessarily empathy in the mutual shared experience, but rather a connection grounded in trust. Yvonne's speaking serves a function: to connect with other people. She explained:

> I don't write. I just… I don't want to. Somebody… ah, people ask me many times after I talk…. I'll tell you why I don't want to write. If I write a story in a book, you may never open the book, and maybe nobody will see the story. But as long as you live you will remember that you met me. You will not forget that. That I was here. That I came. That I told you the whole story of my life. And I do.

It is important to Yvonne that her expressed and articulated experience isn't there to take or leave. She relies on the interpersonal connection to ensure that one hears her, takes her in, remembers her, and accepts that which is being given—her voiced experience.

Contrapuntal Voices

Yvonne's apparent resilience and strength is exemplified through the voices that arose in her interview. The following figure captures Yvonne's voice of elements of her Holocaust experience "within her control," which reveals the many ways Yvonne asserted herself. This voice is characterized by authority, agency, and competence as she demonstrated her "ability to change negative into positive."

Yvonne's voice from "Within Her Control"

Within Her Control
• I thought it was very exotic to live like that [having fled to shack without running water]. • I was having a ball out—with that kind of freedom [after being displaced]. • I had gotten used to being in the country [hiding]. • But I have always been a very grounded kid. • I had become a completely independent individual—a different person in charge, you know. • Life in the convent was OK. I took it very well. I'm very disciplined, as you can see. So I took it fine. • Cleaning the chapel was my favorite place because I was alone. And I could really begin to come to grips with myself which had essentially disappeared from the outside world. Not from me. • And I was a pretty bossy kid, you know. And, people understood they were not messing too much with me. • I know how to do everything. I make all my own things… I know how to shorten pants…I know how to do everything. • And I'll tell you something. I did have thoughts of joining the convent. That's how assimilated to the convent life I had become. • I got married, I had children, I was busy with my life. I had to go to school for a long time … we had two kids at home… I was busy with children, with school, with my profession….that's really my motto: *live your life.* • So I say [to myself], 'don't get scared.' See, there again—that's my character that comes out for me all the time. • I went into [Judaism] like I had gone into Catholicism. The same way. With the same interest, with the same wanting to be a part of it. I was actually repeating something that I had done before. But I was infinitely older.

- I always rise to the occasion.
- I turned it really to a learning experience. Whatever you learn, you turn it into something that you can use. And I said, "That'll never happen again and that's fine.'
- And so that helped me a lot because I could count on myself… a friend said, "you have been victimized, but you are not a victim. You have never been a victim." I have always had [a sense of authority and control].
- I did something that I really enjoyed enormously [when I gave away all of my belongings prior to my move into this studio apartment]. It goes back to being a 12-year-old girl who never saw her home again, never saw my things, my clothes, my friends. Then I went to the convent. The only thing that I took from the convent is what I had in me- in my mind and my heart.
- It gave me the opportunity to start something new. You see, I have the ability to change things from a negative to a positive.
- I reclaimed [my name], because when I got married, you know, I changed my name again. So I took back Yvonne.
- And when [my husband] became sick, I took care of everything. I took over the management of the—the household and everything, you know.

Within Her Control

When speaking about events "within her control," Yvonne's solid identity is evident. She made multiple strong claims and assertions about her personality and character, which she had apparently identified as a child. Yvonne's optimism borders on the overly-positive, especially in the face of aversive and unpleasant circumstances (in a shack, in the convent, scrubbing the chapel floors, giving away her belongings). Her use of the extremely upbeat language, laden with superlatives (e.g.,"very exotic," "having a ball," "very well," "completely independent," "favorite," "really enjoyed enormously") stands in stark contrast to the environment. Yvonne did not simply turn negative into positive, she turned trauma and oppression into favorable adventures. Yvonne located her authority in the face of trauma and operated from a sense of agency, competency, and optimism bordering on fantastic imagination and naiveté.

Yvonne's assertion of her self and agency emerged in many of her I-poems, two of which are included here:

I'm very disciplined
I took
I have
I did

I mean
I was
I was
I was
I could

I am
I kept
I did
I became
I did

The action in this first I-poem is evident ("I took, I did, I became"), as is the self-realization of her potential ("I'm very disciplined, I could"), and her ability to meet that potential ("I did, I became, I did"). Her strong identity is also echoed ("I mean, I am"). Yvonne is in control, self-aware, self-actualized, and happy:

I understood
I was
I know
I said

I grabbed
I pulled
I said
I tried

I actually saw
I used
I tell
I've done
I became

I can

Once again, there is evidence of her strength, her ability to act and manipulate in order not only to survive, but to thrive. Remarkably, even when Yvonne found herself in situations beyond her control, her resilience shone. The figure below captures this resilience as Yvonne voiced her experiences in scenarios where she had no control over what happened.

Yvonne's voice from "Outside of Her Control"

Outside of Her Control
• I did everything I was told to do • So what happened to me, within a very short period, instead of being a child, I became her mother, and I took it on. I took it on like everything else. You know, like the religion. Like the loss of my parents. I couldn't—I didn't put enough together that my parents were not—never come back. For me they were somewhere out there, and they'd all be back, and we'd all be together someday. • No, I wasn't thinking about what I was gonna do about it, because I had gotten accustomed that other people were telling me what to do. And I had no choice. I began to realize that I had no choices anymore. I was in a place. It wasn't bad, and I wasn't unhappy. • And, uh, no I just, uh, I felt I'm here to do what they tell me to do, period. I never looked at the future. • Well, from that moment [when my parents were deported] on, life went on, and it went on for four years. So four years went by. I was in charge by then. I was a 16-year-old with the head of a 30-year-old woman, I would say. I knew everything. I knew what to do. Took care of [my sister]. Kept her clean. Got rid of the lice which invaded her hair and cut her hair short. I did the things that had to be done to keep her going, you know. And for myself, I had almost forgotten who I was by then. I wasn't talking to myself anymore, even when I was alone. • I came with my personality as the older child. And then it was acquired, due to the circumstances, what I had already in me in terms of character was increased, and maybe exacerbated, even, by the circumstances. I had to. Could I tell Father I don't want you to baptize me? I don't want you to change my name? I had no say and no choice. In a situation where you have no choice you do what you have to do.

Outside of Her Control

Although Yvonne found herself subject to the wishes and whims of others, this is not the voice of a victim. She reflected, "I'm not a victim. The pain is there. But I'm not a victim." Instead, one hears the voice of acceptance and compliance. She recognized that her strict circumstances had clear guidelines, which seemed allowed her agency to blossom. She explained that although she had no control over her situation, Yvonne followed the rules, seemingly finding solace in the structure: "I did everything I was told to do," "I'm here to do what they tell me to do, period." She "knew what [she] had to do," and she simply did it.

Yvonne kept her focus on meeting the requirements before her, staying in the present ("I wasn't thinking about what I was going to do about it," "I never looked at the future"). Her gaze became limited to the here-and-now of her situation, and she employed avoidance and fantasy to keep her from being distracted by thoughts of the past or the future ("I didn't put enough together…they were somewhere out there, and they'd be back, and we'd all be together someday"). Yvonne accepted the circumstances as if rising to the occasion ("I took it on"). Her language is evocative of a challenge, one she would face with resolve to do her best, which seemed to serve as an effective coping mechanism that minimized the damage of what many would find to be traumatic events.

Regardless of whether a situation was subject to Yvonne's ability to control or manipulate, she found a way to operate, even excel, within the limits of her circumstances. She noted that her "character was exacerbated" by the circumstances; the seemingly traumatic events of the Holocaust, rather than robbing her of her identity served to strengthen it. Yvonne refused to take on the role of a victim, which is echoed in one of her I-poems:

I mean
I
I cry

I never
I'm not a victim

I get
I look
I
I watch

I want
I
I can say
I'm very happy

Yvonne seems to have coped with potentially traumatic situations by recognizing the things she could change and the things she could not, and to fill out the space granted to her. She was able to act as an agent and exercise control over that which she deemed possible to influence.

Avoidance & Splitting

Yvonne's focus on the present meant she split off her experience from her past, her dreams of her future, and her former identity. The voice below of "avoidance / splitting" reveals how this coping strategy was integral to her resilience.

Yvonne's voice of "Avoidance & Splitting"

Avoidance / Splitting
• But there was a barrier between the outside world and who I am. • [at that time had you stopped thinking about your life before?] Yes. Completely. Completely. We weren't talking about the war. Never. I was in the

moment, and I had plenty to worry about. I had to worry about keeping this little girl in one piece… I worked very hard. There's a wonderful word in French. Being stoic. I was very stoic. I [was] like a steel rod. That's what you had to do.

- I couldn't—I didn't put enough together that my parents were not—never come back. For me they were somewhere out there, and they'd all be back, and we'd all be together someday.
- I went through different kinds of traumas and each one of them dealt with, 'This is the moment.' This is what you do. You know what happened before, but you don't go there. It's too painful.
- But this was a world I couldn't go into because it was just too painful. I had to make a bridge that would not negate what happened—what was—but I would stop thinking about it in the terms in which I was living.
- That [my menses] I never talk about. Because it was so unhygienic that I—I—even that, I blocked that one out. I remember, but like I just remembered—but I wouldn't talk about that.
- This is what I share. It's my life. That's why I can answer any question and I feel OK, except for the ones that I blocked out, which probably are many.
- It depends, you know, as to what you want to bring back and what you don't.
- It was not a time for me to get in there.

Yvonne reveals that she erected a "barrier" and "blocked" out the parts of her experience that were too traumatic in the service of continued coping and maintaining a solid sense of self and purpose in the moment. Again, her narrow focus on the here-and-now was vital, as she shared her mantra: "This is the moment." As Yvonne mentioned, "what you want to bring back and what you don't," her voice of competence and control was evident; she "built a bridge" to the "world" of her trauma and it is her choice about that she "wants" to "bring back" and what she continued to avoid.

While Yvonne describes "blocking" trauma out, she also indicated that she "remembered- but I wouldn't talk about that." Blocking for Yvonne means avoiding discussion of the "blocked out" memory. Yvonne explained that she constructed "a bridge" to that which she wanted to avoid, but one "that would not negate what happened." It is as if she was able to cordon off memories of the past in her mind, knowing she would return to them later. To leave them forever dissociated from her, she believed, would be to deny what happened. Yvonne "couldn't go into" the trauma while she was enduring it; she found ways to leave it, split it off, so that she could return to it later.

Yvonne constructed a self-protective barrier or permeable filter of her own design, again, operating from a place of agency and choice. The sense that this splitting is a function of her own choice is reflected in one of Yvonne's I-poems:

I can
I have
I'm speaking
I'm speaking
I'm involved
I'll tell
I said
I share

I don't share
I can
I feel
I blocked out
I had blocked out
I come across

Although Yvonne indicated that she split off her trauma in an effort to avoid it, she moved in and out, back and forth across the permeable barrier with a fluidity that reiterated a sense of power and control that together can be considered mastery.

Yvonne's ability to move in and out of her trauma was particularly notable as she suddenly changed tenses while telling her story: "Now, one day Mother Superior calls me into the office, and she says… um, 'Yvonne?'—no, 'Mary

Marguerite?' – see? I'm back now. I'm back in my present life. Um, 'your papa is here to pick you up.'" She moved into and out of her story without missing a beat. It is as if she could bring up her memory and experience it in the moment as she told it. This happened multiple times throughout her interview. When revisiting her most horrific trauma, the murder of her dog, she said, "I'm watching this, you know. And I remember the moment as though it was right now. I'm watching this, and I see her. She's talking to the guy." Yvonne's use of the present tense while recounting her past gives the impression that the trauma is happening to her in real time. When telling other traumatic memories, Yvonne said, "I'm telling you all that because it comes back right now."

Even though Yvonne moved into her trauma as if she was experiencing it in the here-and-now, she was able to stay connected to her present-day self, her identity, and to me, her listener. This is a sign that she has mastered her trauma, rather than being victim to an overwhelming re-experiencing of trauma. Yvonne explained how this ability to move back and forth across the barrier of her split off experiences is helpful and indicative of mastery:

> So I sat down. I wrote something for myself, which I will give you. I don't think I was as good in my lecture as I am now. I was not. Because what I can do now is something I couldn't do then. I can keep the story and use the highlights as jumping off points all the time.

The seeming ease with which she tells her story, when coupled with the positive language to describe the sharing of trauma, seems incongruent. Here Yvonne refers to details of her trauma story as "highlights." Again Yvonne glosses over horrific experiences with positive language. At the same time, her description indicated mastery over her trauma. She explained that she went through disruptive work in order to reach mastery:

> And… but it took me a while. I mean, again, it was—the journey that I had gone through had to be retraced—with different appearances. Not different people. But you know, I mean, uh, there's this enormous turmoil of going back now and making peace with what had happened. It's all a lifetime project, you know.

The goal of Yvonne's "project" is to "make peace with what happened." It seems as though making peace for Yvonne is to locate something positive in the experience, even if little positive existed.

Optimism and Humor

Yvonne's optimism and use of humor promoted her connection to others and made her incredibly likeable and easy to be around, but were also baffling and uncanny. These qualities of optimism and humor are central to her coping strategies. Yvonne demonstrated the ability to move very close to her trauma, even experiencing memories in vivo, but then back away, giving herself and her listener a reprieve from the heavy, intense past. Yvonne's humor was playful, which invited her listener to laugh along with her, intentionally lessening the burden that a verbalized trauma can bring to both speaker and listener.

On the surface, Yvonne's humor signaled resilience and interpersonal connection. However, at closer listen, it seemed to serve a secondary purpose. She often joked in the midst of her recounting of her trauma, creating distance from it as if to avoid the horror and painful affect that can accompany the realization of such atrocities. Yvonne's humor in these moments was unexpected and incongruent. For example, when telling of the moment when "the whole world fell apart," Yvonne recalled that she was out in the garden, "probably tyrannizing my sister." When her family fled their home as refugees and were sleeping on the streets, she related that they ended up "in a village with more cows than people." When Yvonne's mother left her in the orphanage to care for her little sister, Yvonne noted, laughing, "I spent the rest of life trying to lose her." She explained: "We all have scars. Believe me. If all my scars were visible, I don't know, I (laughter)—I probably would have to be dressed like a nun." Yvonne related the disturbing memory of first seeing her mother, who had been subjected to horrific medical experimentation:

> She looked like, swollen, and her hair…she had dyed it red. Very short you know. Cut. And I just- I just said to myself, 'Oh, my God.' Now, now I have a father, who, OK, I got used to him, you know? Now I have this strange woman. (Laughter).

Yvonne's laughter is inappropriate given the context. She used humor to back away and protect herself from the atrocity; laughter was an avoidance.

Yvonne's act of negotiating and titrating distance from her trauma through the use of humor allowed her to access the horrific story, making the 'unspeakable' speakable, and then back away when it became overwhelming. She used humor to cope with what many hidden children found traumatic: her religious conversion necessary for hiding:

> And people are always asking me, 'Are you Christian or are you Jewish?' and I say, 'Well, I'm both.' I'm related- by birth I'm related to the Father. By baptism I'm related to the Son. I hope they talk to each other because I have no problem.

Yvonne might have seen her conversion to Christianity as a traumatic transformation in which her Jewish identity was stripped from her. On the contrary, Yvonne saw only the positive: "I'm baptized. Now I have no more—the sins are wiped away. That's what baptism is. It's a wonderful experience that I've had." Her rosy view of her hiding identity ("it's a wonderful experience") stands in contrast to other hidden children, like Fran, who found this imposed identity to be at the very heart of trauma. Yvonne explained that in her hiding identity, her "sins are wiped away." This language is evocative of avoidance, denial, and dissociation; her humor and optimism seem have functioned as tools for avoidant coping. Yvonne's shining optimism is reflected in an I-poem:

I do
I have been blessed
I have been blessed

I'm not sad
I mean
I feel
I sound

I'm
I'm celebrating
I celebrate
I have overcome

Yvonne's repeated assertions of how blessed, happy, and celebratory she is stand in remarkable contrast to the trauma she has endured. She reflected on what she has heard from others that have listened to her traumatic stories:

> 'Yvonne, you're so full of humor.' They say, 'you talk about so serious things but you're so funny and you always have a smile on your face.' It's because I feel that way. I'm happy. I'm blessed. I have wonderful children. Wonderful grandchildren. I am blessed.

Yvonne's incongruencies are recognized, and even applauded, by others. Indeed, while her humor and optimism seem inappropriate in the face of her trauma, these qualities have served her in management of and mastery over her trauma. She continued:

> So, you see, I have been blessed. I have been blessed with—wonderful people come into my life, like you for instance, today, who bring me back to my-- my story—but I'm not sad. I mean, do I feel—do I sound sad to you? No. I'm celebrating. I celebrate my life, which I have overcome some very difficult times, but you know. You know something? It goes back to something I said frequently. If you don't have a choice, make the best of it. Just look for it. Look for the best of what you can do. That will keep you in one piece.

"If you don't have a choice," Yvonne advised, "make the best of it." She has communicated the transformative power of choice, agency, and optimism in effective coping. Her ability to speak about her experiences with authority, competency, and humor, however incongruent, reveals her resilience and mastery over her trauma.

Trauma and Healing

Yvonne witnessed the murder of her dog, was separated from her parents (who then endured "catastrophic" horrors), and was denied her identity as she resided in an orphanage for more than four years. Yet, one does not hear a traumatized individual when listening to Yvonne. Instead, Yvonne's voice is one of striking positives: happiness, gratitude, humor, and optimism. Yvonne explained and demonstrated that even in the face of even the most oppressive circumstances, she found a way to asset control and agency, transforming oppression into opportunity. Although she had to hide, she embraced her new identity and circumstances by narrowing her focus to the present. She split off her past and fears of the future by creating a permeable barrier; she would later return to that which she had split off in order to "make peace" with the traumas she endured. Yvonne employed strong defenses of cheerful optimism and humor that served as antidotes to the pain, effectively creating distance from the trauma.

CHAPTER V

DISCUSSION

Overview of the Study

This study was driven by the question "what is the role of avoidance and expression in coping and recovery from trauma?" This question emerged from a debate in the trauma coping and resilience literature; researchers and practitioners have been increasingly saying that contrary to more than a hundred years of widespread conviction, talking through one's trauma is not always therapeutic (Littleton, Horsley, John & Nelson, 2007). Studies finding evidence of the detrimental effects of debriefing and exposure therapy flew in the face of the primary treatment of PTSD, which is rooted in the notion of processing, integrating, and creating a cohesive narrative about one's trauma (e.g., McNally, Bryant, & Ehlers, 2003; Meichenbaum, 2006; Neimeyer, 2006).

Evidence abounds of the effectiveness of both behavior aimed at expression ("approach" behavior such as facing down, integrating, processing, thinking about, ruminating, and speaking) and avoidance (behavior aimed at inhibiting, repressing, suppressing, ignoring, or refusing to focus on trauma) (e.g., Bonanno, 2004; Feeny & Foa, 2006). What is less clear is why and when these diametrically opposed treatments promote health, and why and when they impede recovery. Developmental and contextual factors are imperative to consider in the treatment of trauma. Children manifest unique and particular trauma reactions, and their coping and recovery styles are necessarily different from adults. Complex trauma in children has major implications for their identity development an is frequently manifested in symptoms of avoidance such as affective inhibition, denial, numbing, and dissociation (Fritsch, 2006; Terr,1991).

Women who survived the Holocaust by hiding their identities are in the unique position to shed light on the developmental and contextual complexities of expression and avoidance in the face of trauma. These women were *hidden children*: Holocaust survivors who were children during the war, saved by the fact that they disappeared into forests, attics, convents, other identities and religions lest they be recognized and persecuted by the Nazis (Tec, 1993). The women interviewed for this study endured a number of traumas: some suffered separation from and loss of their parents and families, some were subjected to the insensitivities and brutalities of those who hid them, many were forcefully displaced to hiding places; all bore witness to genocide of their own people. Without question, these hidden children suffered complex trauma as a result "of long-standing or repeated ordeals" versus an isolated, single trauma (Terr, 1991, p.11).

Despite the variability in their traumatic experiences during the Holocaust, the uniting hallmark of these hidden children was the imperative to be quiet (Fogelman. 1993). Hidden children were mandated to silence their voices, as speaking meant sure discovery of their Jewish identities, and ultimately, death. Their survival literally depended on denial, repression, silence, and avoidance of aspects of themselves. As children, they were at the developmental crossroads where the task at hand is to begin to find one's voice and form a sense of self. Yet the trauma of the Holocaust made this impossible and deadly (Richman, 2006).

Accounts of Holocaust survivors often suggest that there was a period of silence that endured after the war, where those who had suffered did not speak about the Holocaust or express the pain of their traumas (Pennebaker, Barger, & Tiebout, 1989). Indeed, for the women of this study, this was also the case. However, after a latency period of almost forty years, survivors began to come forward and share their stories, giving voice to their trauma (Valent, 1995). What was the function of their silence, and what prompted them to move toward expression? Six women reflect on their experiences of suffering, coping, and recovery from trauma as they ultimately shed light on the function of silence and voice following trauma.

Discussion of the Findings

Two categories of information emerge from the results of this study. The first is comprised of evidence that reiterates the literature reviewed prior to embarking on this study: the impact of trauma on children, the influence of life stage in coping strategies, the importance of generativity and integrity for these survivors, and the role of the empathic listener in healing, to name a few. Indeed, throughout the presentation of the individual narratives, the reader has hopefully been invited to consider the ways in which the individual narratives reiterate concepts initially presented in the review of literature. The second category, however, is the primary focus of this research. This study seeks discovery of knowledge through the logic of induction, allowing new, unanticipated findings to emerge. This discussion, therefore, emphasizes the meaningful new discoveries uncovered in listening to the voices of these participants, rather than summarizing the ways in which the narratives support the literature.

The women of this study give voice to a repetitive injunction against speaking: 1) they were required to silence their identity in order to survive in hiding, 2) they employed defensive metaphorical silencing of the traumatic reality of their Holocaust experiences, and 3) they were silenced by a society who denied them survivor status and did not want to hear about their trauma. The reiterative silencing of each woman's voice is paradoxical. Silence, avoidance and denial saved her life and her psyche, but silence, avoidance and denial robbed her of her identity and sense of self, compounded her trauma, and reiterated her victimhood. The protective mechanisms of silence (survival and buffer from trauma), as well as the injunctions against voice, have rendered the act of speaking loaded and complicated in largely involuntary ways. Thus, even for these women who believe in the benefits of expression, silence pervades. The frame is shifted as the earlier conceptualization of an either/or question (expression vs. avoidance) is no longer relevant. These findings address the more pertinent question: *what is the function of silence and voice for these women who survived trauma*?

Function of Silence

The women of this study survived by being silent. Sonia's narrative, however, first revealed that the silence was much more than a survival strategy; it was also a trauma. In each hidden child's narrative, there are echoes and reverberations of this trauma. The literal denial of one's identity is the most pervasive trauma for these women.

Denial of Self

Sonia survived passing as Catholic. Her father was hidden in the attic of her family's home. To speak, for her, meant certain death both for herself and for her father. Anita was hidden with her family in a barn, mandated to remain utterly silent lest she be discovered and murdered. Connie was hidden with a Christian family, with the Gestapo stopping by for routine checks of homes. Her silence was essential both for the survival of her own family and for the survival of her "hiding family." Fran had her voice silenced when her identity was literally stripped from her; this was essential to her survival, she learned, when she witnessed her school friend being deported for declaring her identity. Reva learned that the forest watchman charged with caring for her was debating whether to kill her lest her voice give them away to the Nazis. Yvonne survived by changing her voice to match the new identity she'd been given in the convent. Silence meant survival; denial of one's true identity was adaptive.

Denial of Traumatic Reality

The traumatic experiences of the Holocaust caused survivors to avoid painful thoughts and feelings in an attempt to escape from the horrors and inescapable, dreadful reality. Generally, child survivors tend to employ avoidance in developmentally-influenced forms: distraction, fantasy, daydreaming, singing, praying, and playing (Klein & Kogan, 1989). Anita gave voice to her own childlike solution: "I found actually a good method. When I had to run away in my dream I used to fly actually. In my dream I would actually fly away." Yvonne would escape in a fantasy world while cleaning the chapel floor. Fran became immersed in religion and prayed. Reva made friends with all of the forest animals. Through prayer, fantasy and play, these children were able to avoid the destructive effects that could occur if one is fully present and aware of the traumas as one is enduring them. Through imagination, they created their own safe and happy worlds that were completely separate from painful reality.

Avoidance continued into young adulthood. The women in this study neither talked about their parents' Holocaust experiences with them, nor do they talk to their children about their own experiences. Sonia didn't talk to her parents about their experiences or her own. Anita divided her life into two tracks: "One track is my Holocaust experience and the other one is my real life with my family." She also explained of another survivor who was speaking at an event, "he didn't want his family to come" hear him talk about his experiences in the Holocaust. Connie explained that the Holocaust was a taboo subject with her children: "we never talked about it." Reva "never could express it with my parents" and likewise states, "I don't like to talk about it with the kids."

Why was there silence between parents and children? Why, in the most intimate circles, was avoidance employed? Reva explained that the intergenerational silence protected her from painful exposure and emotion. She doesn't talk to her children in order to avoid "painful entanglement with my kids." Regarding her parents, she explained, "There was a kind of shame about it, or…I can't even explain the feeling. I couldn't open myself up with them that much."

Anita pondered, "… you show yourself in a very painful way, and I guess we don't like to do that." Exposing trauma within oneself seemed difficult enough; to expose it to others, even family members, was too painful. Yvonne, on the other hand, provided a different explanation: "It was too horrible. I would have done the same as a mother. Now, when I think about it, I wouldn't have told my children. What for? I mean, it was inhuman what happened." Parents' silence may be motivated by a wish to protect one's children from the trauma.

As these women aged, avoidance persisted. Tasks of immigration, marriage, childrearing and career-building provided intense distraction; one could not focus on the trauma of the Holocaust when so busy with life's demands. The challenges of life after the Holocaust were immense for survivors as they attempted to pick up the pieces of their lives, shattered and disjointed from hiding and trauma. The challenges ironically seemed to provide a reprieve from the burden of the traumatic memories. Working as an artist allowed Anita to "blend in" with the crowd and go on as if she hadn't endured trauma, commencing her "real life with my family." Connie explained, "[We were] busy working… and building up a country… we were very busy you know" as young adults having emerged from hiding. This notion pervades today for Connie, though. She continued to site this industriousness as a reason to avoid talking about her trauma even now: "I don't talk/I'm in the midst/I still don't talk/I'm busy." There is an indication that industriousness can serve as an avoidant defense. This was the case for Yvonne as well; her focus on the work at hand gave her "plenty to worry about." She remembered, "We weren't talking about the war. Never. I was in the moment… I had to worry about keeping this little girl in one piece… I worked very hard." These women site busy-ness and productivity as an explanation for why they did not focus on their traumas, and yet it seems that just as easily, it could be the other way around: the busy-ness provides an excuse to not have to face the trauma. In this way, productivity can be seen as an (adaptive) avoidant defense.

Connie described the necessity of avoidance: "You have to have some defenses, too. A little denial, a little avoidance, a little of it all. No… you need a lot. You need- we needed a lot." Indeed, it seems hidden children did need a lot: Reva explained, "I was really completely detached." Fran asserted, "I never talked about it." Yvonne shared, "I would stop thinking about it "I just don't go there." Indeed, even in the interviews conducted for this project, both Connie and Anita chose not to disclose their stories of hiding. Avoidance in adulthood has taken different forms for these women: dissociation from painful affect, deciding to not to talk about the trauma, suppressing thoughts and memories related to the trauma, splitting off and encapsulating the trauma, and diving headlong into work to avoid facing the trauma.

Function of Voice

Speaking, then, has taken on a meaning rooted in the trauma of the Holocaust: it was deadly. Silence, denial, and avoidance enabled literal and psychological survival. Yet all six women endorsed expression as healthy and necessary on the path towards healing. Connie formed support groups that encouraged the sharing of experience and disclosure of trauma because she felt certain that this is what hidden children needed most to recover. Anita, too, participated in groups, and endorsed the sharing of trauma: "Well perhaps if you had an opportunity to speak about them, it may be much more healing than just keeping it in your brain all the time." Sonia's narrative seems to be centered on the notion that giving voice to one's trauma is essential to life. Similarly, Reva espoused her belief that expression is vital: "I would say tell people...because otherwise you are cheating yourself in your life, of your life." Fran has asserted that "speaking was very helpful," and Yvonne has devoted much of her life to speaking about her Holocaust experiences in educational forums and groups. This paradox is at the root of each of these survivor's narratives. Silence both saved *and* threatened, invalidated, split and squelched.

Silence as Trauma

A number of complicating factors have been identified as making complex trauma more challenging for children, including, importantly, underdeveloped cognitive skills with which to make sense of the trauma (Scheidlinger & Kahn, 2005; Williams, 2006). While the women in this study may not have been able to make coherent sense of their traumas at the time of the Holocaust, they were able to recognize and understand that they were being traumatized. The adults in their lives had seemingly not accounted for this capacity for traumatization in children. Sonia explained, "my parents sort of acted as if I was so young I couldn't possibly remember or deal with these things" even though "it was always accessible to me." The misassumption that children couldn't understand their trauma seems to have been translated as a harmful, invalidating message: *You are not a survivor.*

Anita explained, "With the young ones it was even worse because the notion was when you're young you don't remember." Connie, too, gave voice to this experience: "'Oh your mother suffered' and the kids didn't. That was the implication." This misconception about the capacities of children in the face of trauma served to intensify the traumatic effects and further confuse the children, perpetuating the silence imposed on their experiences.

In the "hierarchy" of survivorship, hidden children had no place. They were denied status as Holocaust survivors. Sonia received the message that it was imprudent to claim that she had been traumatized in the Holocaust, thus, "I didn't see myself as a survivor for many years." Anita explained that as hidden children, "we were just so different that there was no support to make it legitimate, so to speak." The societal message was: "a Holocaust survivor was a concentration camp survivor." Each woman in this study reflected her belief that "no one wanted to hear about" her painful experiences in the Holocaust. Time and time again we hear the women tell of a society (family, friends, therapists, acquaintances) that turned its collective back on the suffering of these hidden children, unable or unwilling to hear them give voice to the trauma. Connie expressed the pain and frustration, and invalidation she experienced in the face of this imposed silence: "I think I had enough of being- not being recognized as having suffered." Again and again, Reva communicated the horrific nature of trauma as if she needed to repeatedly assert her status as a trauma survivor. Yvonne's discovery that others had been traumatized as hidden children was "a revelation." The imposed silence encouraged these survivors to leave their traumas split off rather than expressed, explored, and integrated. It perpetuated the trauma, keeping these women hidden beyond the duration of the Holocaust.

Effects of Silence

Judith Herman (1992) has written about the silencing power of an uninterested socio-political climate: "after every atrocity one can expect to hear the same predictable apologies… in any case it is time to forget the past and move on" (p.8). She describes how survivors "complain bitterly that no one wants to know the real truth." Dr. Herman continues, "When the victim is already devalued (a woman, a child), she may find that the most traumatic events of her life take place outside the realm of socially validated reality. Her experience becomes unspeakable" (p.8). The unspeakability of the trauma has resulted from society's deaf ears. Each of the women in the present study point to those in their social circles, immediate and extended, who are hard-of-hearing regarding their trauma.

In Dana Crowley Jack's (1991) investigation of depression in women, she discovers, "the loss of self coincides with a loss of voice in relationship. Voice is an indicator of self. Speaking one's feelings and thoughts is part of creating, maintaining, and recreating one's authentic self" (p.32). The survivors in this study, faced with the injunction against speaking about their identities and experiences, lost cohesion of the self. As children, these girls experienced the silencing of their voices at the very life phase in which finding a voice is crucial for development. While they should have been tackling the developmental tasks of identity formation, gaining an understanding of a self in relation to others, they were mandated to create a parallel, inauthentic self that denied their true identities.

Splitting

Victims of a reiteratively imposed silence, these women's selves were split as children: Jewish/Christian, past/present, feeling emotions/numb, traumatized self/normal self. For Sonia, splitting meant disconnecting her emotions from the rest of the psyche, so that thinking and feeling did not coexist. Anita found that splitting her trauma ("shutting it off") from the rest of her life allowed her to remain in connection with others, safe as part of the crowd. Connie split off the trauma she endured and deemed it invalid. Fran's world was split into two: the "false" life under imposed disguises and the "real" life which was stripped from her. Reva's trauma created an enduring split, a parallel though unreconciled self from which she speaks half of the time. For Yvonne, splitting meant "blocking out" that which she did not wish to remember. She glorified that which had been painful and traumatic, unable to see it as "bad." While splitting occurred as a defense in the face of trauma, it also occurred as a consequence of hiding and having been silenced. The injunction against speaking cleaved the psyche; splitting was the wound.

Passing

How can these women speak about their traumas, especially after having silence repeatedly imposed on them? They have survived by hiding, passing as someone other than themselves. Judie Alpert (2009) has written about passing, which she identifies as a "masking" an "obscuring" of one's past in order to "evade categorization." She explores how society often mandates that individuals pass lest they experience marginalization or become ostracized altogether. Dr. Alpert references the passing of African Americans as white, the passing of homosexuals as "straight," and the passing of chronically ill as well. These hidden children, too, are arguably passing. Some of the women of this study continue to hide, masking their identities as survivors and obscuring their traumatic pasts, despite believing in the therapeutic value of speaking. Having split themselves into "normal" and "traumatized" selves, they attempt to operate from the "normal" self even when they do not feel "normal," lest they be categorized by others as damaged. They have interpreted that there is an implicit societal message that no one wants to hear about it. The relationship between shame and silence is made clear when one considers the societal messages communicated to survivors. Amongst other hidden children, however, they do not have to pass; they can tell their stories without fear of shame or being ostracized.

Informing the Debate?

Coping with trauma, as initially conceptualized in this study, is a choice between avoidance and expression. Underlying this conceptualization was the assumption of volition. The very term "avoidance" implies choice. As these women explored the function of silence and voice in their experiences of trauma, it quickly became clear that while both coping strategies were integral in each survivor's experience, the strategies were rarely consciously employed. For these women, silence was a mandate and an injunction. Silence arose from a lack of cohesion and identity. Avoidance, denial and splitting were involuntary responses to the trauma. These narratives reveal that as Erikson's and Life Span theories suggest, the women were pulled toward integration in later stages of life, facing and expressing their trauma. But this, too, seemed to be out of one's aegis. For some, it was a celebrated right to tell one's story, for others it was a painful, involuntary pull. Anita explained adroitly, "it just says 'hello, I'm here.'" The assumption of choice in coping with trauma undermines the true trauma for these women: the injunction against speaking and the denial of identity.

Implications

The most painful and pervasive trauma for these six women is seems to be the denial of identity and subsequent silencing of the voice. While the women interviewed for this study are not representative of hidden children as a population, much less of complex trauma survivors as a whole, their voices can inform our understanding of the suffering and recovery of these populations. Denial of identity and silencing of voices are traumas that unfortunately occur for multiple groups of individuals, including sexual, ethnic, and religious minorities, immigrants, those threatened by genocide, those suffering from mental and physical illness; the list, sadly, goes on and on. Based on the narratives of these survivors, those struggling with an injunction against speaking are likely suffering- in as complex and varied ways as these hidden children.

While a lack of choice and agency characterizes the traumatic experiences of such populations, these survivors have given voice to aspects of their lives that have proven therapeutic: finding solace and affinity in a group, being listened to empathically (but only when ready to speak), and even employing powerful avoidance strategies to move forward with the task of rebuilding one's life. One thing seems certain: with the trauma of having identities imposed on them, it is imperative to let the coping strategies be dictated by the survivor. These survivors have expressed that there is no right answer in coping with trauma; avoidance and expression are dictated by complex forces, many of them out of the control of the traumatized individual. For them, the time for talking was highly idiosyncratic. While opportunities to voluntarily express should be offered to survivors of trauma, only under their aegis will interventions be truly therapeutic.

This study only begins to illuminate the experiences of female survivors of complex trauma. Indeed, the results here provide more questions than answers: What is the impact of silence on the developmental task of identity formation for females? What is society's role in silencing of its traumatized citizens? In what ways is trauma perpetuated or compounded by the bystander's reactions to it? What happens to marginalized members of a society when two diametrically opposed societal messages aimed at them collide (*we don't want to hear it* vs. *speak out*)? How can one heed the broader societal push to speak out after having been conditioned for silence for so long? In what ways do women's experiences of silence and voice regarding trauma differ from those of men? While the arguments between the theoretical camps are both informative and valid, they have not fully addressed these survivors' experiences of coping. To understand the integral roles of both silence and voice, we should turn our ear to the true experts: those who have lived the experience and know firsthand of the function of coping strategies in the face of trauma. Let their wisdom not fall on deaf ears.

Limitations

The epistemological assumptions underlying this research provide both the strengths and the limitations of this study. This study sought to capture the phenomenology of coping and recovery for hidden children of the Holocaust. Underlying this undertaking is the assumption that there is no objective reality, but rather multiple perspectives on reality that are subjectively formed in relation to one's context, Zeitgeist, gender values, and cultural norms. Instead, the researcher operates from the post-positivist stance that an objective reality can never be perfectly apprehended; an individual's experience of the events of her life necessarily colors her understanding and recall of these events. Here, the researcher strived to understand the survivors' experiences through an interpretive framework that depends on co-construction of knowledge between two people. Of course, the historical event of the Holocaust is an objective reality, but how the hidden child experienced this reality is at the heart of this research.

Of the two paradigms in research, qualitative and quantitative, the quantitative paradigm is most concerned with establishing a causal relationship between variables, and clarifying the extent of that causality. The qualitative paradigm, as has been applied here, is more concerned with the process; how one variable is related to another (Maxwell, 1996). The two camps of literature reviewed within this study both assert that one coping style (avoidance or expression) can predict psychological health and well being, revealing the key to recovery from trauma. However, this study was not concerned with some objective notion of truth or finding the "answer" to the problem. Instead of discerning the "best" style, the variable that inevitably leads to mental health, the goal of this study was to examine the process by which individuals cope and the ways in which they experienced recovery (Maxwell, 1996). These survivors' narratives helped to create a crystallized view, according to a variety of different perspectives, of healing from trauma (Perlesz & Lindsay, 2003).

While each camp (expressors vs. avoiders) argues for its own apprehensible truth, this is a paradox. There can be no "right answer" because knowledge is subjective and constructed by the individual through an interpretive framework. Therefore, expressing might work for some people some of the time in some conditions, just as avoidance might operate similarly. Such strategies are subjective. How the survivor interprets the effectiveness of these and other coping strategies and co-constructs this knowledge with the researcher is of interest in this study (Perlesz & Lindsay, 2003). The interpretation of this knowledge is an inherently interpersonal process and can never be replicated. This study, in some ways, is similarly a paradoxical proposition: these narratives are highly-individualized and not meant to be generalized, yet they provide helpful insight into the treatment of other traumatized populations.

The researcher's orientation as a critical theorist welcomes the examination of her own bias and subjectivity. The Listening Guide, the method of data analysis for this study, welcomes this examination as well. In a relational setting such as the semi-structured interview employed here, the survivor's narrative exists within a relational framework between the interviewer and interviewee. This co-researching relationship cannot be free from subjectivity of either person in the relationship. By taking this notion into account through the methodological framework employed here, a richer and more nuanced picture of coping and recovery emerges as the interviewer and interviewee co-construct knowledge.

Given this notion of co-construction of reality, this study is inherently limited by its subjectivity. The relationship I formed with each of the interviewees necessarily impacted both what the hidden child said and how I listened. The words of my participants have been filtered through my own lens- complete with my biases- in the process of analysis. Therefore, their narratives are limited by my own understanding of what they've shared. In the service of transparency, I disclosed the "Roots of My Question" as an admittance of my own bias. However, despite this disclosure, the lack of generalizability is inherent; these narratives can never be replicated and are highly idiosyncratic.

The epistemological underpinnings of this proposal clarify the lack of generalizability of this study, and the lack of desire for generalizability in this study. The goal of this research was to advance an analytic goal and to understand the process of the individual's experience from a variety of unique perspectives. This study was limited by a small number of unique perspectives. Despite the small number of participants in this study, the notion of triangulation still proved useful. In triangulation, the researcher sought to understand this data in relation to the existing bodies of literature on both expression and avoidance. The researcher moved back and forth between the existing theories on expression and avoidance in light of the knowledge gained by the survivors' narratives. This served to improve the researcher's interpretive power in the analysis of the narratives (Sandelowski, 1995).

This study was also limited by the bias inherent in the participants; all were affiliated with the Hidden Child Foundation; this group's major thrust is speaking out about trauma. The voices of those survivors who choose not to speak about their trauma are not heard in this study. While potentially valuable participants, those survivors who are truly avoiding are, by definition, unlikely to speak about their Holocaust experiences, even if only in terms of coping styles. Thus, this study did not include any self-described avoiders.

While this study seeks in part to understand the evolution of the individual's coping and recovery styles over time, no longitudinal data was collected for these participants. Multiple standpoints across the lifespan are not taken into account. Rather, individuals were asked at a discrete point late in their lives to explain their pathways since childhood. Participants' accounts of their Holocaust experiences and life since rely on memory, which has been demonstrated to be particularly fallible with regards to trauma (DeBellis, 1999). Finally, this study is limited to the study of women's accounts of coping and recovery. As gender necessarily impacts both experience of trauma and coping strategies, there are expected differences with regards to the research question. These differences are not addressed within the scope of this study.

www.ingramcontent.com/pod-product-compliance
Lightning Source LLC
LaVergne TN
LVHW010059170826
845678LV00012B/2178

* 9 7 8 8 2 3 6 5 1 9 6 8 8 *